Mennonite Confession of Faith

Mennonite Sources and Documents

Editorial Council

Noah G. Good	James O. Lehman
Amos B. Hoover	John L. Ruth
S. Duane Kauffman	David J. Rempel Smucker
Albert N. Keim	A. Grace Wenger
Christian J. Kurtz	Carolyn C. Wenger

Managing Editor
Irvin B. Horst

No. 1
Tennessee John Stoltzfus:
Amish Church-Related Documents
and Family Letters
by Paton Yoder

No. 2
Mennonite Confession of Faith
Adopted April 21st, 1632, at Dordrecht, the Netherlands
by Irvin B. Horst

Published by
Lancaster Mennonite Historical Society
Lancaster, Pennsylvania

Mennonite Sources and Documents

No. 2
Mennonite Confession of Faith
Adopted April 21st, 1632, at Dordrecht, the Netherlands

by Irvin B. Horst

Mennonite Confession of Faith

Adopted April 21st, 1632, at Dordrecht, the Netherlands,
and Widely Accepted in Germany, France, Colonial Pennsylvania,
the United States, Canada, and Elsewhere

Newly translated and edited
with prefatory materials in English for the first time

by Irvin B. Horst

Lancaster Mennonite Historical Society
Lancaster, Pennsylvania
1988

Published by the Lancaster Mennonite Historical Society,
2215 Millstream Road, Lancaster, PA 17602-1499

Manufactured in the United States of America
Design by Paula M. Johnson
Printed by Mennonite Publishing House, Scottdale, Pa.

Library of Congress Catalog Card Number: 87-80243
ISBN:0-9614479-6-6

Table of Contents

Acknowledgment

The only recorded copy of the first edition of the Dordrecht Confession of Faith, *Confessie ende Vredehandelinge* (Haarlem, 1633), exists in the Amsterdam Mennonite Library (Doopsegezinde Bibliotheek), now placed in the University of Amsterdam Library (Universiteits Bibliotheek), located at Singel 425, Amsterdam. We gratefully acknowledge permission from both libraries to make use of this rare book and to reproduce it here in facsimile reprint.

Foreword

The Dordrecht Confession of Faith is a peace agreement produced by the Dutch Mennonites in 1632. In Europe and America it has long been a bulwark for Mennonites to inform their governments about their faith, especially in matters relating to the swearing of oaths, military service, and the payment of taxes. Simultaneously the document has served as a handbook for Mennonite leaders to instruct newcomers to the faith. Ever since the colonial period this confession has been the most commonly used document among Mennonites in North America. It is still consistently used by conservative groups such as the Old Order Amish and Old Order Mennonites.

Thus the importance of the Dordrecht Confession grew beyond the Netherlands. Eventually the Swiss Brethren accepted it, and in time significant use of the confession shifted from the Dutch to the ethnically Swiss Mennonites. Several Swiss Brethren refugees in Alsace first accepted it in 1660. In 1664 it was first published in German. Consequently, its use spread rapidly over the German-speaking areas of central Europe.

Early in the course of the Mennonite settlements in Pennsylvania, the church leadership requested translation and publication of the Dordrecht Confession in English. These publications appeared in 1712 and 1727 in order to introduce Mennonite beliefs to the English government and to soften anti-German tensions with English neighbors. The 1727 publication included a statement made by a 1725 ministerial conference, possibly held at Germantown, Pennsylvania. It was signed by sixteen Mennonite leaders who stated:

> We the hereunderwritten servants of the Word and God, and elders in the Congregation of the People called, Mennonists, in the Province of *Pennsylvania*, do acknowledge, herewith make known, That we do own the afore-going [Dordrecht] Confession . . . and [have taken] the same to be wholly ours.

The above statement thus indicates universal acceptance of the Dordrecht Confession by the Pennsylvania Mennonites.

This new translation was made by Irvin B. Horst, presently living in his native Lancaster County, Pennsylvania, where he is employed by the Lancaster Mennonite Historical Society. He has collected Mennonite books over the years and has channeled hundreds of rare volumes into Mennonite libraries in this country. He also taught Anabaptist and Mennonite history in Virginia for ten years and in the Netherlands for eighteen years. He has the unusual Anabaptist perspectives and the rare linguistic abilities needed to accomplish this translation task successfully. Previous translations were grammatically heavy because they seem to have been based on the German translation. We owe him a debt of gratitude, for this project has been in various stages of negotiation and production since 1981. He also has included a list of 255 known editions. These stand as a silent testimony to the extensive use and importance of the Dordrecht Confession in the Mennonite world during the past three and one-half centuries.

The Lancaster Mennonite Historical Society, resolved to make Mennonite source materials available, is most pleased to present this new product to its members, to the church at large, and to the general public. Also, the Society is grateful for the moral and financial support of this project by interested persons and especially for the gift of funds from Eastern Mennonite Associated Libraries and Archives. Hopefully this form of the Dordrecht Confession will enrich the faith of its readers, emphasize its spirit of love and reconciliation, and ultimately give glory to the supreme God on high.

—Amos B. Hoover
January 1, 1987

Editor's Introduction

If we examine the Dordrecht Confession as it appears in the *Martyrs Mirror*, we find that Van Braght presents it as one of three Dutch Mennonite statements of faith. They are: *Scriptural Instruction* of 1627 (better known as the *Olijftacxken*, the small Olive Branch, first printed in 1629); *Confession of Faith and the Principal Articles of the Christian Doctrine* of 1630 (also known as the *Corte Confessie*, the Short Confession of Jan Centsz); and the Dordrecht Confession of 1632 (first printed in 1633).[1] All three have much in common, especially with regard to the distinctive Mennonite doctrines, including shunning, although Dordrecht has separate articles on the ban and shunning and was in general the most conservative of the three. At a meeting at Haarlem in 1649—as Van Braght relates—all three were "adopted without contradiction as a unanimous confession."[2]

Thus after its initial importance as a separate confession among the Flemish Mennonites, the Dordrecht statement functioned in the Dutch brotherhood chiefly in relation to the other two mentioned above. Not only in 1649 but at Haarlem again in 1651, at Leiden in 1660, and at Utrecht in 1661 the three confessions were considered as one. In 1665 they were brought together along with the Concept of Cologne and published under the title *De Algemeene Belijdenissen* (the General Confessions, in the sense of the common confessions).[3]

It is often emphasized that the Dordrecht Confession along with other contemporary statements are significant chiefly as instruments of church unity, as a means of restoring fellowship among the various branches of the Dutch

---

[1]Thieleman J. van Braght, *The Bloody Theater or Martyrs Mirror of the Defenseless Christians* (Scottdale: Mennonite Publishing House, 1950), pp. 27-44. At the beginning of the second part Van Braght includes the Old Frisian confession of faith, "Confession of Faith, According to the Holy Word of God," the so-called Thirty-Three Articles, written by Pieter Jans Twisck, pp. 373-410.

[2]Van Braght, *Martyrs Mirror*, p. 27.

[3]*De Algemeene Belydenissen der Vereenigde Vlaemsche, Vriesche, en Hooghduytsche Doopsegesinde Gemeynte Gods* (Amsterdam: 1665).

Mennonites. This motivating force should be duly recognized, especially as the occasion for writing them, but even in their origin and composition the creedal aspect took an all-important place. This aspect became more and more prominent as the confessions functioned in the life of the Mennonite church in the Netherlands and in other countries. We may obtain some insight into this aspect by examining Van Braght's presentation of the three confessions under the subject heading "Succession of Doctrine." After printing the text of the Apostles' Creed, he follows with the Mennonite statements. He views them as a continuation of apostolic faith and says of them: "in which confessions the creed set forth above is more fully interpreted and explained."[4] In this way Van Braght asserts the ongoing tradition of the apostles' doctrine.

Van Braght is known to us today chiefly as the author of the *Martyrs Mirror*. But we should not overlook the importance of his leadership role during the middle decades of the seventeenth century and especially his firm stand for the maintenance of apostolic doctrine. Born in 1625, he was only seven years old when the Dordrecht Confession was adopted at his home town. However, he was ordained as a minister in the united Flemish wing at the age of twenty-three (1648) and soon became known as a capable preacher and proponent of the Mennonite faith. His name is on the list of leaders attending the second meeting at Haarlem (1651) pertaining to the confessions, and he served as chairman in 1660 at Leiden. Four years later he died at the age of thirty-nine.

The separate history of the Mennonite confession we commonly designate today as Dordrecht is limited in its Dutch form to the original edition of 1633 and to a reprint at Rotterdam in 1658. A reading of the introduction, here printed in English for the first time, reveals how closely the statement was related to the Peace Agreement reached between the Oude Vlamingen (Old Flemish, the conservative wing) and the Jonge Vlamingen (Young or New Flemish, the more progressive wing). Only when both parties acknowledged their mistakes and asked for mutual forgiveness was it possible to bridge the breach.

It is significant that twice the Agreement is referred to as "our Brotherly Union." Is this an allusion to the *Brüderlich Vereinigung* of Schleitheim (1527)? A Dutch translation of the *Brüderlich Vereinigung* appeared in the Netherlands in 1560 so that it is entirely possible that the memory of this early work, formulated at a time of disunity, was revived at Dordrecht. In both instances of 1527 and 1632 we learn much about the occasion for a statement of faith from a long introduction but very little about how the articles were drawn up—whether or not discussion and compromise took place. Also, in both cases the authorship is not explicitly stated although it is rather certain that Michael Sattler wrote the *Brüderlich Vereinigung*, and Adriaan Cornelisz, the Eighteen Articles. Adriaan was an elder in the congregation of the Old Flemish at Dordrecht. He died in 1632, the year of the Agreement.

The Dordrecht meeting, coming somewhat more than a century after Schleitheim, took place openly and in public. We have more documents relating to it. We know, for example, that the town authorities were somewhat hesitant to give permission for a gathering of many "Anabaptist" leaders to take place within their walls. The date had to be

---

[4]Van Braght, *Martyrs Mirror*, p. 27.

changed at least once. We know, too, that some of the Flemish leaders did not attend, especially those from the northern provinces of Friesland and Groningen. Evidently the Flemish from Franeker, the seat of much division, also were not represented. Some leaders aggressively opposed the meeting, and at least two of them traveled to Dordrecht to hinder or stop the proceedings but were held back at the doors of the church.[5] More positive is the information about meetings of thanksgiving for the newly attained unity. At Haarlem the euphoria was so great that it led to the compilation and publication of a new hymnbook based on the Eighteen Articles: *Fondament, ofte de principaelste liedekens over de poincten des Christelijcken geloofs* (The Foundation, or the most essential hymns pertaining to the points of the Christian faith) (Haarlem, 1633).[6]

This may be the place to note that, although we have translated *Vredehandelinge* in the title and *Vrede-Handel* in the preface as "Peace Agreement," there are some nuances of meaning in the original words which should not be overlooked. The use of the ban and the practice of shunning had become so notorious because of their frequency and misuse that they became known as *handel* (business or trade). It should not be forgotten, however, that the initiative or procedure in disciplinary matters was called a *handeling* (action, proceeding). In the prefatory parts of the Eighteen Articles the usage of these terms tends to be ironical, but with the prefixing of *vrede* (peace) an effort is made to give a legitimate word a more positive turn.

The translation offered here is not a paraphrase of the original text. Rather, it is a direct translation of the full text with an attempt to make it readable in modern English. In general I have retained the paragraphing but have frequently given the long, convoluted sentences in shorter units of declarative statement. The titles of the articles do not appear in the original and thus are placed here in square brackets. The side notes of the original consist entirely of scriptural references. All of these have been checked and placed next to the paragraphs to which they apply. (In the preface the references have been included in the text as was the case in the original.) The reference to 4 Esdras in Article II has been retained even though this apocryphal book is now considered spurious.

The justification for this new edition arises from both scholarly and spiritual considerations in the life of the church. Most evident are the prefatory materials which appear here for the first time. One senses that the time has arrived when they should be studied and pondered among Mennonites in North America as well as by other churches not only for the light they throw on the Eighteen Articles but also for the purpose of resolving disunity in the life of the church.

---

[5]W. J. Kühler, *Geschiedenis van de Doopsgezinden in Nederland II, 1600-1735*. Eerste Helft (Haarlem: 1940) pp. 193-195.

[6]The existence and true identification of this book has recently been established by the research of Drs. Pieter Visser, a doctoral student at the University of Amsterdam. I am indebted to him for sharing his discovery with me. In *The Mennonite Encyclopedia*, s.v. "Fondament," by Van der Zijpp, the author was aware of the existence of this hymnbook but noted: "no copy has been found as yet." For many years a copy was in the Mennonite Library at Amsterdam. However, it was attributed to Pieter Jans Twisck, and its relationship to the Dordrecht Confession had been forgotten.

Additionally, at a time when the continuity of faith is often not understood or appreciated, it may be worthwhile to recall and reflect upon how our Dutch forebears in a context of great economic prosperity and cultural flowering decided to remain steadfast in the doctrine of the apostles. Something of this loyalty and vitality as reflected in the Eighteen Articles appealed to Mennonites in other lands and times, and it accounts, no doubt, for the document's widespread acceptance.

There are lesser matters chiefly of a textual nature which the careful student will note by way of comparison. Through the centuries portions have been added to and subtracted from the text.[7] Adaptations also occurred. The scripture references have not always been consistently presented. Although the respect for textual accuracy has varied, the desire to retain the essence of statement has been rather constant. A text of any kind is bound to suffer from the process of translation so that it would be fool-

hardy to claim that the English text on the following pages transmits the full meaning of the original—not to mention the felicity of the Dutch phrasing.

The inspiration for this undertaking came from the remembering at Amsterdam and Lancaster that in 1982 the Dordrecht Confession had been in existence for 350 years. The conversations which ensued and the requests for translation and bibliography led to the results on these pages. After some delay it has now been possible to conclude at Lancaster the tasks begun at Amsterdam. The Lancaster Mennonite Historical Society through its board and staff has given much encouragement by way of personal interest and efforts toward publication. I want especially to thank my wife, Ava, for much good and expert assistance.

—Irvin B. Horst
August 8, 1986

---

[7]The most obvious example is to be found in the editions published at Basel, Switzerland, which added a nineteenth article pertaining to the Holy Spirit. See nos. 15 and 16 in the appendix.

Brief Bibliography
of Secondary Sources

Hoover, Amos B. "350 Years since the Dordrecht Confession of Faith," *The Jonas Martin Era, Presented in a Collection of Essays, Letters and Documents that Shed Light on the Mennonite Churches during the 50 Year Ministry (1875-1925) of Bishop Jonas H. Martin.* Denver, Pa.: Amos B. Hoover, 1982, pp. 958-979.

Horst, Irvin B. "The Dordrecht Confession of Faith: 350 Years," *Pennsylvania Mennonite Heritage* 5 (July 1982): 2-8.

Loewen, Howard John. *One Lord, One Church, One Hope, and One God: Mennonite Confessions of Faith in North America: An Introduction.* Text-Reader Series, no. 2. Elkhart, Ind.: Institute of Mennonite Studies, 1985, pp. 24, 26-27, 62-70.

Studer, Gerald C. "The Dordrecht Confession of Faith, 1632-1982," *The Mennonite Quarterly Review* 58 (October 1984): 503-519.

Wenger, John Christian, "The Dordrecht Confession," *The Doctrines of the Mennonites.* Scottdale, Pa.: Mennonite Publishing House, 1951, pp. 77-87.

Zijpp, N. van der. *De Belijdenisgeschriften der Nederlandse Doopsgezinden.* Haarlem: 1954.

Note

A recent text edition and study of the Dordrecht Confession has appeared in the Netherlands: "Confessie van Dordrecht 1632, bewerkt door J. Brüsewitz m.m.v. M. A. Krebber, ingeleid en toegelicht door I. B. Horst en S. Voolstra," *Doperse Stemmen*, no. 5. Amsterdam: Doopsgezinde Historische Kring, 1982.

IV.
Confeſſie
Ende
Vredehandelinge/
Geſchiet tot Dordrecht/ Aº. 1632.
den 21ᵉⁿ. April/ tuſſchen de Doops-ghelinde
diemen de Vlaminghen noemt : Waer-
in een yder kan ſien ende mercken/
hoe eñ waer op dat deſen Vrede gemaeckt eñ be-
veſtight is.

Matth. 5.9.
Salich zijn de Vrede-maeckers/ want ſy ſullen Godts kin-
deren ghenaemt worden.
Hebr. 12.14.
Haeckt nae den Vrede ende Heylichmaeckinghe / ſonder de-
welcke niemandt den Heere ſien en ſal.
1 Corinth. 7.15.
Godt heeft ons in Vrede gheroepen.

TOT HAERLEM,

Ghedruckt by *Hans Paſſchiers van Wesbuſch*, Boeck-drucker
op 't Marckt-veldt inden beſlagen Bybel. 1633.

This title page of the first edition of the Mennonite Confession of Faith, adopted at Dordrecht in 1632 but first printed at Haarlem in 1633, is reproduced from the copy in Doopsgezinde Bibliotheek (Mennonite Library) at the University of Amsterdam.

Confession and Peace Agreement

Reached at Dordrecht, Anno 1632, on the 21st of April,
between the Mennonites [Doopsgezinden] called the
Flemish: in which everyone can see and perceive how and
on what this peace has been made and established.

Matthew 5:9
Blessed are the peacemakers: for they shall be called the
children of God.

Hebrews 12:14
Follow peace with all men, and holiness, without which no
man shall see the Lord.

I Corinthians 7:15
God hath called us to peace.

HAARLEM
Printed by Hans Passchiers van Wesbusch, Printer
at the Marcktveldt in den beslagen Bybel, 1633.

Preface to the Peace Agreement
Reached Among the Mennonites Called the Flemish
on April 21, 1632, at Dordrecht

indful and peace-loving reader, seeker after happiness and truth, we hear daily of some persons who are not favorable to our peace agreement. Failing to comply with the nature of love, which sees the best in everything, they do not speak well of it. Thereby they cause innocent and unlearned persons—who regrettably at times are more impressed by men of today than by the teaching and life of our Savior Jesus Christ and his beloved apostles—to shy off and to turn away from it. These opponents not only reject us but also the peace so highly commended by the Son of God and his apostles. They do not obey, it seems, the exhortation of Christ: "Blessed are the peacemakers: for they shall be called the children of God," Matt. 5:9. "Follow peace with all men, and holiness, without which no man shall see the Lord," Heb. 12:14. "Have peace one with another," Mark 9:50. "On earth peace," Luke 2:14. "Peace I leave with you, my peace I give unto you," John 14:27. "How beautiful are the feet of them that preach the gospel of peace, and bring glad tidings of good things," Rom. 10:15 and Isa. 52:7. "Behold, how good and how pleasant it is for brethren to dwell together in unity! It is like the precious ointment upon the beard, even Aaron's beard: that went down to the skirts of his garments; as the dew of Hermon, and as the dew that descended upon the mountains of Zion: for there the Lord commanded the blessing, even life for evermore," Ps. 133. "If it be possible, as much as lieth in you, live peaceably with all men," Rom. 12:18. "For the kingdom of God is not meat and drink, but righteousness and peace, and joy in the Holy Ghost," Rom. 14:19. "Let us therefore follow after the things which make for peace, and things wherewith one may edify another," Rom. 14:19. "God hath called us to peace," 1 Cor. 7:15. "Finally, brethren, farewell. Be perfect, be of good comfort, be of one mind, live in peace; and the God of love and peace shall be with you," 2 Cor. 13:11.

Taking these and other scriptures for our learning to heart and considering them in the fear of God, we found that we had strayed from them and, in so doing, had left the way of peace. Like David in Ps. 119:59 we thought about our ways and found it high time to return to the instruction of the Lord, to humble ourselves before God and our brethren, and to say with Jeremiah in Lam. 3:42: "We have transgressed and have rebelled: thou hast not pardoned." With our minds kindled by this and opening our hearts with Lydia, Acts 16:14, we sensed that the time had come to re-establish the broken peace. We desired to live and walk again in peace and love with each other, with the scattered sheep—of whom we were not the least—who are one with us in faith, doctrine, and practice and in this way magnify God's great and holy name. We undertook this then for the upbuilding and betterment of our own ways, for the edification of our fellowmen, and finally for the common salvation of our souls. We trust that the merciful God—who is a God of peace rather than of wrangling and discord—will give his gracious blessing through his blessed Son, our Savior and Lord. Apart from him we can do nothing, John 15:5. Amen.

For the reason mentioned at the beginning of this preface, we could not neglect to inform all true lovers of peace and at the same time to make public in what capacity and upon what articles of faith the peace is again built and established—at Dordrecht, on April 21, 1632, the peace was renewed and took place by a mutual, complete forgiving of, freeing from, and acquittal of all previous faults and mistakes, wrong actions, and restrictions—that no one from now on through ignorance should speak unjustly about something of which he is not informed. Use what follows for your profit.

—In Haarlem
as of April 8, [1633],
by a Lover of Peace.

Introduction

Brethren, we along with our elders and ministers (unworthy as we are) of the united church of God here at Dordrecht; also, we, the undersigned elders, ministers, and brethren—who as co-workers were invited, delegated, and came, each for himself and for his church—are gathered in the Lord's name in the church at this place and are one with it: wish heavenly wisdom, divine enlightenment from the almighty, eternal, and incomprehensible God for all churches, coworkers, brethren, and partakers of our common Christian faith in all towns and places where this—our brotherly union, appeasement, and agreement—will be presented and read. May this divine wisdom enable you to test, discern, and pursue what is necessary for our common peace and mutual improvement. Such peace is pleasing to God, agreeable to men, and enables us to walk as becomes our calling. In order that we and you with us after this life, along with all God's chosen, holy, and beloved saints, may be eternally saved through our Lord Jesus Christ. To this end may the kind and faithful God help us and grant his gracious blessing to make you and us worthy and acceptable. Amen.

Further, this must be mentioned: it is public knowledge for quite some time in many or at least some places that for various reasons an unhappy contention leading to confusion—yes, even separation and schism—rose and continued among fellow believers of the same persuasion and brotherhood of faith. Not the least among these contentions was the division of the House-Buyers which continued for many years. As a result of this and all that developed from it, God's worthy name was slandered and disgraced, and the church became an object of reproach and contempt. Along with this there was much giving and taking of offense as well as provocation and insult, especially in the church at Franeker but also elsewhere. One might well lament such matters with regret and remorse and wish they had never happened. Mistakes are usually better seen and discerned afterwards than before as is the case with these contentions. The more one considers them, especially with an impartial mind, the stronger one is convinced that the cause as well as the unfortunate results cannot entirely be laid at the feet of one side. Both sides have been greatly at fault; both have been overzealous and immoderate in the use of discipline, of rejection and separation from each other.

Both sides lacked a recognition of love as the principal garb and characteristic of the true followers of Christ. Love is the sum of the great commandments, the fulfillment of the law (John 13:35; Col. 3:14). Love is indeed the bond of perfection; it binds believers in a harmonious relationship with the Lord; it binds believers as one heart and soul to each other in peace and unity. As members of one body they are closely related to each other at all times and in every way: to bear and forgive the shortcomings of each other (Luke 6:36), to cover the failures of neighbors. They deal gently with each other, showing compassion and mercy; they do not increase the hurt of the injured nor oppress or reject the weak (2 Cor. 5:11; Ezek. 34:4). Instead each esteems the other person more than himself (Phil. 2:3), and in this way the weaker members receive attention and respect (1 Cor. 12:23). Indeed, love was too much lacking on the part of both sides and much unhappiness, strife, and contention were the result.

If this bond of love becomes weak and cold—or actually broken by many—the enemy sows tares [seeds] in the hearts of many dozing members (Matt. 13:25) which take root in bitterness. All kinds of confusion and error result and bear fruit such as envy, discord, backbiting, hate, and strife. As a tiny spark, if it is fanned and not extinguished in time, can cause great destruction, so it has gone in this matter. Also, one may truthfully say that not the House-Buyers only, nor only the results of this affair and all that was attached to it, but much rather the sins of both sides should be acknowledged as contributing to the cause of the contention.

All of this we here at Dordrecht as well as brethren at many other places have taken to heart and given thought and considered. In this we profit from the many excellent examples in Scripture, how the patriarchs and prophets, along with the apostles as shepherds, fathers, and leaders in the church, truly sought the unity of fellow believers. Their instruction is given to us as pointers so that we can see as in a mirror how we ought to act and treat each other in matters of contention and disagreement. We see in this mirror their endeavors to meet each other with respect. These fathers and leaders have highly recommended all Christian believers to follow them in such matters as they followed the great Shepherd (Heb. 13:20). With these examples before us to follow, quarreling, wrangling, backbiting, and destruction ought finally to cease. We should now accept each other in loving kindness and in trust. Yes, meet each other in love and peace (Ps. 85:11). As much as possible should be done to seek the lost (Matt. 18:12), to bring together those scattered and gone astray, to bind up the wounded (Ezek. 34:16), to repair the breaches (Isa. 58:12), to level the hills and remove the rocks of offense, to repair the roads and make a straight path so that on it the wayfaring man shall not err (Isa. 35:8). Always on every occasion we must seek what is pleasing to God, what is necessary for the welfare of the church, as well as what makes for peace and healing among each other.

We of both sides have earnestly prayed to God and constantly labored that what happened and continues to happen in the dispute over the House-Buyers be brought to an end: that following the example of the patriarchs, according to the teaching of Scripture, we might again meet each other in love, reconciliation, and unity. Finally, by the grace of God and with his help it was possible that we together in mutual agreement, representing both sides, the one as well as the other from many different places, were called by letter to come to Dordrecht.

And so both sides assembled here in the Lord's name (unworthy as we were) in love and friendship. Insofar as it was fitting, we have spoken about and discussed these matters in the fear of the Lord. After this we turned to prayer and supplication, for which the Lord had prepared our hearts so that we were inclined towards each other. For this be the praise and thanksgiving only to him. Unshackled, free, and unbound as we had now been made, with sincere confession of guilt in regard to the matter mentioned above, we also set free and unbound all those whom we and our former leaders, together with their congregations, had bound, banned, or burdened in any way.

And moreover, in sincere repentance and contrition we begged each other for forgiveness; thereafter we forgave each other and acquitted each other of everything which had been done by us or our former leaders or the congregations involved, specifically or in a general way in regard to the matter of the House-buying at Franeker. This included everything connected with it whether words, acts, books, letters, or any form of mistreatment or indebtedness— nothing excepted—wherever up until now we together as a group or separately as individuals of either side had grieved, hurt, or offended others.

In regard to this matter we have also at the same time together in sincere and earnest confession prayed and implored our merciful God and heavenly Father in the name of his dear Son, our Lord Jesus Christ, for complete forgiveness of everything done until now in this matter by us and our brethren on both sides (Matt. 6:12; Prov. 28.9). We desired complete forgiveness for everything we have in any way done against God in his majesty or against each other or any other person.

In evidence and confirmation of this complete agreement, reconciliation, and unity, we have received each other with the hand and with the brotherly kiss of peace. Each accepted the other in the name of the Lord as is becoming for those who are bound to each other in one fellowship with him.

In this union we have accepted and included all fellow members, present and absent, both as a group and as individuals, those residing here as elsewhere, those invited as well as all others—excluding none. Just as we included those who were with us, the invited and their proxies, and who stand with us united in goodwill, doctrine, and practice, we have not overlooked those who hereafter wish to follow our example and thus live to the honor of God and for the upbuilding, edification, and improvement of the church so that together we might with heart and soul live and walk peaceably (Acts 4:12). Such a walk becomes our calling and is in keeping with our common Christian faith, the principal articles of which are briefly drawn up— from the Word of God—and here added.

Article I
[God and the Creation]

The Principal Articles of Our Common Christian Faith as Taught and Practiced by Our Church

Scripture testifies that without faith it is impossible to please God, for everyone who comes to him must believe that he is and that he rewards those who seek him. Therefore, we confess with the mouth and believe with the heart—in company with all devout men and women and in keeping with Scripture—in one eternal, almighty, and incomprehensible God: the Father, Son, and Holy Ghost. There is only one God—none other before him and none other after him—for from, by, and in him are all things. All praise and honor be to him forever. Amen.

Heb. 11:6; Deut. 6:4; Gen. 17:1; Isa. 45:9; 1 John 5:7; Rom. 11:36.

We believe and confess that this one God is the creator of all things, visible and invisible. During six days he created the heaven and earth, the sea, and everything in them. We also believe that he continues to rule and maintain his creation by his wisdom and by the power of his word.

1 Cor. 12:6; Gen. 1; Acts 14:15.

And when he had completed his work in keeping with his good pleasure and had ordered it as perfect and right, each part in keeping with its nature and being, he also created the first man, Adam, the father of us all. He gave him a body made from a lump of clay and breathed into his nostrils the breath of life. Thus Adam became a living soul from God, created in his own image and likeness in true righteousness and holiness unto eternal life. God regarded him as above all other creatures and adorned him with many great and glorious gifts. He placed him in the delightful garden, or Paradise, and gave him a command and a prohibition. After this he took a rib from Adam, made a woman of it, brought her to him, and gave her to him as a helper, companion, and wife. Accordingly, God caused that from this first man, Adam, all men living on the entire earth have generated and descended.

Gen. 1:27; 2:7; 5:1; 2:17-18; 2:22; Acts 17:26.

Article II
[The Fall of Man]

We believe and confess, according to Scripture, that our first parents, Adam and Eve, did not continue long in the happy state in which they had been created. They became disobedient and broke God's high command, for they were seduced and misled by the snake and the malice of the devil. In this way sin entered the world, and death by sin has passed upon all men, for all have sinned and incurred the wrath of God and fallen under his commendation. Therefore, Adam and Eve were driven by God from Paradise or the delightful garden to cultivate the earth, in sorrow to provide for themselves, and to eat their bread in the sweat of their faces—until they returned to the earth from which they came. We believe that through this one sin they fell so deeply, became estranged and separated from God, that neither they themselves, nor any of their posterity, nor angels, nor any other creature in heaven or earth could help them, redeem them, or reconcile them to God. They would have been eternally lost had not God in compassion for his creatures intervened in his love and mercy.

Gen. 3:6; 4 Esd. 3:7; Rom. 5:12, 18; Gen. 3:23; Ps. 49:7; Rev. 5:1-5; John 3:16.

Article III
[The Restoration of Man]

We believe and confess that God—notwithstanding the fall of the first man and his descendants, their sin and wrongdoing, and their helplessness to save themselves—did not abandon men and women to be cast off entirely nor to be eternally lost. No, God called them back to himself again; he comforted them and showed them that there was yet a means of reconciliation. This was the unspotted Lamb, the Son of God, who was prepared for this purpose before the foundation of the world. While our first parents were still in Paradise, he was promised for consolation, redemption, and salvation to man and his posterity. In truth, he was granted to them by faith from that time on so that all of the devout patriarchs, to whom this promise was often renewed, have longed for, desired, and seen by faith its fulfillment. They knew that his coming would save and free men and women from their sins, guilt, and unrighteousness and restore them again to God's favor.

John 1:29; 1 Pet. 1:19-20; Gen. 3:15; 1 John 3:5; 2:1; Heb. 11:13, 39; Gal. 4:4.

Article IV
[The Coming of Christ]

We also believe and confess that when the time of the promise came and was fulfilled—the time so much longed for and awaited by all the devout patriarchs—then the promised Messiah, Redeemer, and Saviour, going out from God, was sent into the world. This was in keeping with the prediction of the prophets and the witness of the Gospel writers. Yes, came in the flesh and revealed himself: the Word itself became flesh and man. He was conceived in the virgin Mary (who was engaged to Joseph of the house of David); and when she gave birth to him as her firstborn at Bethlehem, she wrapped him in swaddling clothes and laid him in a manger.

John 4:25; 16:28; 1 Tim. 3:16; John 1:14; Matt. 1:22; Luke 2:7, 21.

We believe and confess that he is the same one whose origin is from of old, from the days of eternity; his years have no beginning, his life, no end. Of him it is testified that he is the Alpha and the Omega, who is, was, and is to come. He is the one who was forseen, promised, sent, and came into the world; he is God's own, first, and only Son. He was before John the Baptist, before Abraham, before the world; yes, he was David's Lord and the God of all the world. He is the first-born of all creatures who was sent into the world and yielded up the body prepared for him as an offering and sacrifice whose fragrance was pleasing to God. This was for the solace, redemption, and salvation of all men and women, for the whole human race.

Mic. 5:2; Heb. 7:3; Rev. 1:8; John 3:16; Heb. 1:16; Rom. 8:32; John 1:30; Matt. 22:43; Col. 1:15; Heb. 10:5.

But as to how and in what manner this body was prepared, how the Word became flesh, and he himself man, we are content with the explanation given by the faithful Gospel writers. Therefore, we confess with all the saints that he is the Son of the living God. In him is all our hope, comfort, redemption, and salvation, and we should not seek the same in any other.

Luke 1:30-31; John 20:31; Matt. 16:16.

Further, we believe and confess with Scripture that, when he had finished the work for which he had been sent into the world, he was—in keeping with the providence of God—delivered into the hands of evil men; that he suffered under the magistrate Pontius Pilate; that he was crucified, died, and was buried. On the third day he rose from the dead and ascended to heaven and took his seat at the right hand of the throne of Majesty in the heavens. From that place he shall come again to judge the living and the dead.
Luke 22:53; 23:1; 24:5-6; 24:50.

The Son of God also died, tasted death, and shed his precious blood for all men; in this way he bruised the serpent's head, destroyed the works of the devil, cancelled the bond which pledged us to the decrees of the law, and achieved the forgiveness of sins for the entire human family. Thus he effected salvation for all, from the time of Adam to the end of the world, who believe in and obey him.
Gen. 3:15; 1 John 3:8; Col. 2:14; Rom. 5:18.

Article V
[The Law of Christ]

We also believe and confess that before his ascension Christ set up and instituted his new covenant. And because it was to remain an eternal covenant—which he confirmed and sealed with his own precious blood—he highly charged and commissioned that it not be altered, neither by angels nor men, nor be added to nor diminished. And since it contained the whole counsel and will of his heavenly Father as far as is necessary for salvation, he has caused it to be published by his dear apostles, messengers, and servants, whom he has called and chosen for that purpose. He sent them to every part of the world to preach in his name to all nations, people, and tongues, proclaiming repentance and forgiveness of sins. Accordingly, he has declared in his covenant that all men without distinction as his children and lawful heirs, insofar as they follow and live up to its precepts by faith, are not excluded from this glorious inheritance of salvation. Excepted are the unbelieving and disobedient, the obstinate and unrepentant, who despise such salvation by their sinful actions and thus make themselves unworthy of eternal life.
Jer. 31:31; Heb. 9:15-17; Matt. 26:28; Gal. 1:18; 1 Tim. 6:3; John 15:15; Matt. 28:19; Mark 16:15; Luke 24:46-47; Rom. 8:17; Acts 13:46.

Article VI
[Repentance and Amendment of Life]

We believe and confess, since man is by nature inclined to do evil from his youth and is prone to sin and wickedness, that, therefore, the first lesson of the new covenant of the Son of God is repentance and amendment of life. Men and women with ears to hear and minds to understand should show the fruits of repentance and amend their lives. It means to believe the Gospel, to depart from evil and do good, to cease to be unjust, and to reject sin. In short, it implies a discarding of the old nature with its deeds and putting on the new nature, which is created after God in righteousness and true holiness. For neither baptism, nor the Lord's Supper, nor church membership, nor any other outward ceremony can without faith, the new birth, and the amendment of life make it possible for us to please God and to receive the solace and promise of salvation. With sincere hearts and completely by faith we must come to God and believe in Jesus Christ as Scripture speaks and testifies of him. By this faith we receive forgiveness of sins, are justified and sanctified, and are made children of God—yes, partakers of his image, nature, and being: born again from above by the incorruptible seed.

Gen. 8:21; Mark 1:15; Ezek. 12:1; Col. 3:9-10; Eph. 4:21-24; Heb. 10:21-22; John 7:38.

Article VII
[Baptism]

With regard to baptism we believe and confess that all penitent believers who by faith, the new birth, and the renewing of the Holy Ghost are made one with God, their names written in heaven—upon a Scriptural confession of faith and amendment of life—ought to be baptized with water in the name of the Father, the Son, and the Holy Ghost. This is in keeping with the doctrine and command of Christ and the practice of his apostles: for the burial of their sins and in order to become incorporated into the fellowship of the saints. In consequence of this they must learn to keep all that the Son of God taught and commanded his followers.

Acts 2:38; Matt. 28:19-20; Rom. 6:4; Mark 16:16; Matt. 3:15; Acts 2:38; 8:12; 9:18; 10:47; 16:33; Col. 2:11-12.

Article VIII
[The Church of Christ]

We also believe and confess: a visible Church of God—namely, of those who, as explained above, truly repent, believe rightly, and have received true baptism. They are united with God in heaven and incorporated into the fellowship of the saints on earth. These persons we hold to be the chosen race, the royal priesthood, the holy people, who have the witness that they are the spouse and bride of Christ. Indeed, they are children and heirs of eternal life, a tent, a tabernacle, and house of God in the Spirit, built upon the foundation of the apostles and the prophets—Christ being the chief cornerstone. This church of the living God he bought and redeemed with his own precious blood. According to his promise, he will always stand by this church: to comfort and protect even to the end of the world. He will dwell and walk with her and keep her so that neither floods, nor tempests, nor even the gates of hell shall ever move or conquer her. This church is to be known by her Scriptural faith, doctrine, love, and godly life; also by a fruitful living up to, use, and observance of the ordinances of Christ which he so highly commended and enjoined upon his followers.
1 Cor. 12:13; 1 Pet. 2:9; John 3:29; Rev. 19:7; Titus 3:6-7; Eph. 2:19-21; Matt. 16:18; 1 Pet. 1:18-19; Matt. 28:20; 2 Cor. 6:16; Matt. 7:25; 16:18.

Article IX
[The Choosing and Ministry of the Teachers, Deacons, and Deaconesses in the Church]

With regard to offices and election in the church, we believe and confess—since the church can neither exist and grow nor continue as a structure without offices and ordination—the Lord Christ himself as a father in his own house has instituted offices and ordinations and regulated how each should walk in this respect in keeping with his own work and calling and do that which is right and necessary. For Christ himself as the faithful, chief shepherd and bishop of our souls was sent and came into the world, not to wound or to break or to destroy the souls of men but to heal and cure, to seek the lost, to break down the barrier and dividing wall, to make one out of two, and thus to

gather Jews, Gentiles, and people of all nations into one fold—that is, one fellowship in his name. For this he gave his life so that none should go astray; thus he made a way for their salvation by redeeming and releasing them when there was no one to help or assist.
Eph. 4:10-12; 1 Pet. 2:25; Matt. 12:20; 18:11; Eph. 2:14; Gal. 3:28; John 10:9; 11:15; Ps. 49:7.

We also believe that before his departure Christ provided for his church faithful ministers, apostles, evangelists, pastors, and teachers—whom he had chosen by the Holy Ghost with prayer and supplication—to feed his flock, to govern the church, to watch over and nurture her, and in every way care for her—yes, to do in all things as he had done before them by way of example and precept.
Eph. 4:11; Luke 10:1; 6:12-13; John 2:15; Matt. 28:20.

Also, that the apostles likewise, as faithful followers of Christ and leaders in the church, were diligent with prayer and supplication to God to provide from among the brethren: bishops, pastors, and leaders for all the cities and places where churches existed; to ordain such persons who took heed to themselves, to the doctrine, to the church and who were sound in the faith, godly in life and conduct with a good reputation within as well as without the church. That so they might be an example, light, and pattern in all godliness and good works; that they might worthily administer the ordinances of baptism and the Lord's Supper. And that they might appoint in all places faithful men as elders capable of teaching others, ordaining them by the laying on of hands in the name of the Lord to enable them to minister to the church according to their ability that as

faithful servants they might invest their Lord's talent, gain by it, and consequently save both themselves and those who hear them.
1 Tim. 3:1; Acts 1:23-24; Titus 1:5; 1 Tim. 4:16; Titus 2:1-2; 1 Tim. 3:7; Luke 19:13; 2 Tim. 2:2; 1 Tim. 4:14; 5:2.

And that they also should diligently see to it, each where he has oversight, to provide in all places deacons to look after and minister to the poor that they might receive gifts and alms and in turn faithfully distribute them, with all honesty as is becoming, to the saints in need.
Acts 6:3-6.

Also, that honorable, older widows should be chosen and ordained as deaconesses for the purpose of assisting the deacons to visit, comfort, and provide for the poor, infirm, ill, and distressed. Also, they should visit widows and orphans in order to comfort and care for them; further, to help look after the necessities of the church according to the best of their ability.
1 Tim. 5:9; Rom. 16:1; James 1:27.

What further concerns the deacons, that they, especially those gifted and chosen from the church for this purpose and ordained—to help lighten the work of the bishops—may also admonish and assist in word and doctrine in order to serve one another in love with the gift they have received from the Lord. So that through the mutual service and assistance of every member, according to his ability, the body of Christ may be improved and the Lord's vineyard and church may increase in growth while keeping the structure properly in order.

Article X
[The Lord's Supper]

We also believe in and observe a breaking of bread or Lord's Supper such as the Lord Christ Jesus instituted with bread and wine before his suffering. He ate it with his apostles and commanded it to be done in remembrance of himself. Accordingly, his apostles also taught and observed it in the churches and commanded the believers to do it in memory of the Lord's death and suffering, that his body was broken and his precious blood shed for us and for all mankind. Remembering also its effect—namely, the redemption and salvation he accomplished—which showed us sinful men such a love whereby we are highly admonished to love and forgive each other and our neighbor as he has done unto us. Also, to keep in mind and to practice the unity and fellowship we have with God and each other, a unity represented and signified in the breaking of the bread.

Matt. 26:25; Mark 14:22; Acts 2:42; 1 Cor. 10:16; 11:23-26.

Article XI
[Footwashing]

We also confess a washing of the saints' feet just as the Lord Christ instituted and commanded but also exemplified by washing his apostles' feet himself even though he was their Lord and Master. This was an example that they should wash each other's feet. They followed this example and taught the believers to observe it as a sign of true humility; also as a special sign of the true washing by which we are washed in his precious blood and our souls are cleansed.

John 13:4-17; 1 Tim. 5:10; Gen. 18:4; 19:2.

Article XII
[The State of Marriage]

We believe and confess that in the church of God there is an honorable state of marriage between two free and believing persons in keeping with and as God originally ordained in Paradise and established himself between Adam and Eve. And likewise the Lord Christ approved it and removed all the abuses which had gradually crept in by restoring it to its first order. The apostle Paul also taught and permitted marriage in the church leaving it to everyone's free choice to marry in the Lord in keeping with the original plan. By the phrase "in the Lord" we think it ought to be understood that, as the patriarchs were to marry among their own relatives or kindred, no other liberty is granted to the believers of the new covenant. They are to marry among the chosen generation and the spiritual kindred of Christ (and none other), those who have been united to the church as one heart and soul, having received baptism and standing in the same fellowship, faith, doctrine, and walk before they are united in marriage. Such are then joined together in his church, according to the original ordinance of God. This is called "marrying in the Lord."

Gen. 1:27; 2:18-24; 1 Cor. 7; Matt. 19:4-6; 1 Cor. 9:5; Gen. 24; Gen. 28; 1 Cor. 7:39.

Article XIII
[The Office of Civil Government]

We also believe and confess that God instituted civil government for the punishment of evil and the protection of the good as well as to govern the world and to provide good regulations and policies in cities and countries. Therefore, we may not resist, despise, or condemn the state. We should recognize it as a minister of God. Further, we ought to honor and obey it and be ready to perform good works in its behalf insofar as it is not in conflict with God's law and commandment. Also, we should be faithful in the payment of taxes and excises, giving what is due to the state as the Son of God taught, practiced, and commanded his disciples to do. Besides, we should constantly and earnestly pray for the state and the welfare of the country that under its protection we may lead a quiet and peaceful life in all godliness and honesty. And further, that the Lord may be pleased to reward them here and in eternity for all of the privileges and benefits as well as the liberty we enjoy here under their laudable rule.

Rom. 13:1-7; Titus 3:1; 1 Pet. 2:17; Matt. 17:27; 22:17-21; 1 Tim. 2:1-2.

Article XIV
[Defense by Force]

With regard to revenge and resistance to enemies with the sword, we believe and confess that our Lord Christ as well as his disciples and followers have forbidden and taught against all revenge. We have been commanded to recompense no man with evil for evil, not to return curse for cursing, but to put the sword into its sheath or in the words of the prophet beat the swords into plowshares. From this we understand that following the example, life, and doctrine of Christ, we may not cause offense or suffering but should instead seek to promote the welfare and happiness of others. If necessary for the Lord's sake, we should flee from one city or country to another; we should suffer the loss of goods rather than bring harm to another. If we are slapped, we should turn the other cheek rather than take revenge or strike back. In addition, we should pray for our enemies and, if they are hungry or thirsty, feed and refresh them and thus assure them of our good will and desire to overcome evil with good. In short, we ought to do good, commending ourselves to every man's and woman's conscience, and, according to the law of Christ, do unto others as we would wish them to do unto us.

Matt. 5:39, 44; Rom. 12:14; 1 Pet. 3:9; Isa. 2:4; Mic. 4:3; Zech. 9:8-9; Matt. 5:39; Rom. 12:19-21; 2 Cor. 4:2; Matt. 7:12.

Article XV
[The Swearing of Oaths]

Concerning the swearing of oaths, we believe and confess that our Lord Christ forbade it and taught his followers that they should not swear at all. Rather, they should let their yes be yes and no, no. From this we understand that all oaths, great or small, are prohibited. Instead, all our promises, commitments, and contracts, yes, also our statements and bearing of witness, ought to be confirmed only with our word—yes in what is yes, no in what is no—provided that at all times we keep our word and live faithfully as if we had confirmed and established it with an oath. And if we do this, we have confidence that no man, not even the magistrate, will have just reason to lay a heavier burden on our mind and conscience.
Matt. 5:34-35; James 5:12; 2 Cor. 1:17-18.

Article XVI
[Excommunication or Separation from the Church]

We also believe and confess a ban, separation, and Christian punishment in the church for amendment and not for destruction: whereby the pure may be distinguished from the impure. In other words, if anyone, after he is enlightened, has attained knowledge of the truth, and has been received into the fellowship of the saints and afterward either willfully or out of presumption against God or otherwise falls back into the unfruitful works of darkness by which he is separated from God—so that the kingdom of God is denied him—that such a person, after the matter is made public and sufficiently known in the church, may not remain in the congregation of the righteous. As an offensive member and public sinner he ought to be set aside, punished before all, and purged as bad leaven: this for his amendment and as an example and warning to others; also that the church may be kept pure and free of scandals so that the name of the Lord be not dishonored and the church be not an offense to those who are without. Finally, a sinner should not be condemned along with the world but that he may be convinced in his heart and mind and again brought to contrition, repentance, and amendment of life.

Isa. 59:2; 1 Cor. 5:5-6, 12; 1 Tim. 5:20; 2 Cor. 10:8; 13:10.

Concerning brotherly reproof and exhortation and also the instruction of those who err, it is necessary to use all diligence and care in watching over them and admonishing them with all meekness with a view to their correction and amendment; and in case any should remain obstinate and unconverted, to reprove them as seems fit. In short, the church ought to put away from their company those who are evil—whether in doctrine or in life—but no other.

James 5:19-20; Titus 3:10; 1 Cor. 5:12.

Article XVII
[The Shunning of the Excommunicated]

With regard to the withdrawal from or shunning of the separated, we believe and confess that, when someone has so far fallen away either by his wicked life or false doctrine so that he is estranged from God and as a consequence justly separated from and punished by the church, such a person must be shunned according to the doctrine of Christ and his apostles and avoided without partiality by all members of the church (especially by those to whom it is known). In eating and drinking and other similar fellowship such a person should be shunned and avoided so that one is not involved with his way of life or a partaker of his sins. This should be done so that the sinner may be ashamed, struck in his heart and conscience, and thus be induced to an amendment of his ways. Such a shunning,

we believe, ought to be used in Christian moderation so that it may have the effect not of destroying but of healing the sinner. If he is in need, hungry, thirsty, naked, ill, or in any form of want, then we ought—according to the love and teaching of Christ and his apostles—to help and give him assistance. Otherwise, the shunning leads to ruin instead of correction or amendment. Such persons should not be considered enemies but should be admonished as brethren. Again, the purpose is to bring them to acknowledgment, contrition, and repentance of their sins in order that they may be reconciled to God and again received into the church. In this way love can have its way with them as is becoming.

1 Cor. 5:9-11; 2 Thes. 3:14; Titus 3:10.

Article XVIII
[The Resurrection of the Dead and the Last Judgment]

As to the resurrection of the dead we believe and confess in keeping with Scripture that all men who have died and fallen asleep shall be awakened, made alive, and raised up on the last day by the incomprehensible power of God. These together with those who are then alive shall be changed at the sound of the last trumpet and appear before the judgment seat of Christ. There the good shall be separated from the evil so that everyone may receive in his own body according to his deeds whether they be good or evil. The good or the devout shall be taken up with Christ as the blessed, enter into life eternal, and receive that joy which no eye has seen nor ear heard to reign and triumph with Christ forever. On the other hand, the wicked or the ungodly shall be driven away as accursed and thrown into great darkness, into the eternal pains of hell, where in the words of Scripture the worm dieth not and the fire is not quenched. There they shall never have any hope, comfort, or redemption. May the Lord by his mercy make all of us fit and worthy that no such thing befall any of us but that we may take heed to ourselves and be diligent so that at that time we may be found before him in peace, without spot, and blameless. Amen.

Matt. 22:30-31; Dan. 12:12; Job 19:26-27; John 5:28; 2 Cor. 5:10; 1 Cor. 15; Rev. 21:11; 1 Thess. 4:13; 1 Cor. 15:51; Mark 9:44.

These now, as briefly stated above, are the principal articles of our common Christian faith as in our church and among our people are taught and practiced. They are, according to our judgment, the only true Christian faith, which the apostles in their time believed and taught. Yes, they testified to this faith with their lives and confirmed it with their death; some of them sealed it with their blood. With them and all godly men and women we seek in our weakness to abide by the same in life and death that by the grace of the Lord with them we may obtain salvation.

It was decided that two exact copies, signed by us as principals of the meeting, should be kept as a matter of record—one to be retained here at Dordrecht and the other, at Amsterdam. Also, that all elders now present at this meeting should receive a copy to show at home. Furthermore, that each elder obtain a copy for the congregations he serves.

So, beloved fellow workers, brothers and sisters, and all companions in Christ, we trust that with this short, written explanation our efforts and work in this matter, carried out in love, will be understood. To this end we humbly pray and sincerely request that you will accept this from us (unworthy as we are) for the good and will follow the same in love and that you willingly and in good faith will let it serve you together for your deepest peace and betterment. So that in this way also, the God of peace will dwell in and abide with you and us together, according to his promise; and that the good work begun may continue to bring honor and glory to the Lord, that it may serve for the growth and upbuilding of his church. To this end and further in everything that is necessary and pleasing to him, the good and merciful God will help us and you, granting his gracious blessing and strengthening and approving our efforts that we together may be made worthy and able. Amen.

We request, pray, and desire in all friendliness that everyone, and in particular those who receive our above-mentioned statement in their hands or obtain knowledge about it by way of seeing, hearing, or reading—and find they cannot accept, approve, or see through it in all its parts—that in such cases you still will always speak well of it to others. One should recall that it has been written: he who speaks well of a matter (and explains all with a good interpretation) such a one in turn is well spoken of. To recall also that God's Son has charged and commanded: whatsoever ye would that men should do to you, do ye even so to them.

As notice, witness, and full confirmation of what was transacted and done here by the congregation and our countrymen together as stated above: Thus we the undersigned elders, ministers [dienaren], and brethren as such and in the name of and in behalf of the request of this, our as now united congregation at this place, as also for ourselves and in behalf of each congregation, the same as our public and general Brotherly Union, Pacification, and Agreement, have endorsed and undersigned. Use it for your benefit. And hereby we commend you to God Almighty in his gracious keeping unto salvation. Sincere greetings with the everlasting peace of the Lord from all of us and from the congregation here. Amen.

Transacted and concluded in our united congregation in the town of Dordrecht, April 21st, Anno 1632. New Style. Farewell.

And was signed by

Dordrecht.
Isack de Coningh, and in behalf of our ministers, Ian Jacobs.

Middelburg.
Bastiaen Willemsen.
Ian Winckelmans.

Vlissingen.
Oillaert Willeborts.
By Iacob Pennen.
Lieven Marijness.

Amsterdam.
Tobias Govertsz.
Pieter Iansen Moijer.
Abraham Dirckxsz.

Haarlem.
Ian Doom.
Pieter Grijspeer.

Bommel.
Willem Iansen van Exselt.
Ghisiert Spiering.

Rotterdam.
Balten Centen Schoenmaker.
Michiel Michielsz.

Dordrecht.
By me, Hans Cobrijssen.

By me, Iacuis Terwen.
Claes Dircksen.
Mels Ghijsbaerts.
Aeriaen Cornelissoon.

From the Upper Country.
Peeter van Borsel.
Antonij Hansz.

Crefeld, ditto
Herman op den Graff.
Weylm Kreynen.

Zeeland.
Cornelis de Moir.
Isaac Claessen.

Haarlem.
Dirck Wouters Kolenkamp.
Pieter Ioosten.

Rotterdam.
Israel van Halmael.
Heyndrick Dircksz. Apeldoren.
Andies Lucken, de Jonghe.

Schiedam.
Cornelis Bom.
Lambrecht Paeldinck.

Leyden.
Mr. Christaen de Coninck.
Ian Weyns.

Blokzijl.
Claes Claessen.
Pieter Peters.

Zierkzee.
Anthuenis Cornelisz.
Pieter Iansen Timmerman.

Utrecht.
Herman Segerts.
Ian Hendricksen Hoochvelt.
Daniel Lhorens.

Amsterdam.
David ter Haer.
Pieter Iansen van Singel.

Gorinchem.
Iacob van der Heyde Sebrechts.
Ian Iansz. vande Cruysen.

Arnhem.
Cornelijes Iansen.
Derojck Rendersen.

Utrecht.
Abraham Spronck.
Willem van Broeckhuysen.

IV.

Confessie

Ende

Vredehandelinge/

Geschiet tot Dordrecht/ Aº. 1632.
den 21en. April/ tusschen de Doops-ghesinde
diemen de Vlaminghen noemt : Waer-
in een yder kan sien ende mercken/
hoe eñ waer op dat desen Vrede gemaeckt eñ be-
vestight is.

Matth. 5. 9.
Salich zijn de Vrede-maeckers/ want sy sullen Godts kin-
deren ghenaemt worden.
Hebr. 12. 14.
Jaeckt nae den Vrede ende Heylichmaeckinghe / sonder de-
welcke niemandt den Heere sien en sal.
1 Corinth. 7. 15.
Godt heeft ons in Vrede gheroepen.

TOT HAERLEM,

Ghedruckt by *Hans Passchiers van Wesbusch*, Boeck-drucker
op 't Marckt-veldt inden beslagen Bybel. 1633.

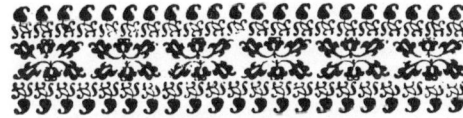

VOOR-REDEN,

Op den Vrede - handel tot Dordrecht Anno 1632. den 21. April,
tusschen de Doops-ghesinde, diemen de Vlamingen noemt,
gheschiedt:

Endachtige, Vreedlie-
vende, heyl- eñ- waer-
heyt-soeckende Leser:
Alsoo ons dagelijcx ter
oorē komt , dat eenige menschē die
onsen Vrede niet seer toegedaen en
zijn , en derhalven na den aerdt der
Liefdē, die alle dingē tē bestē duyt,
daer het beste niet van en spreeckē,
waer deur sy de simpele eñ eenvou-
dige herten (die somtijts (het welck
te beklagē is) meer sien op menschē
die teghenwoordich zijn , als op de

(§ 2)   Lee-

Leeringhe eñ het Leven van onſen Heylant eñ Salichmaker Ieſus Chriſtus ende ſijn lieve Apoſtelen) niet alleene van ons , maer oock van den Vrede, die ons van den Sone Godts ende ſijn Apoſtelen ſo hooge bevolē is, af-keerigh ende ſchuw maecken: de welcke (ſoo't hem laet aenſien)te weynich nadencken ende in achtinge nemen de reden Chriſti Mat.5.9: Salich zijn de Vrede-makers , want ſy ſullen Kinderen Godts ghenoemt worden ; Hebr. 12. 14 : haeckt nae den Vrede ende Heylichmaeckinghe , ſonder de welcke niemandt den Heere ſien en ſal ; Marc. 9.49 : hebt Vrede onder malkanderen ; Luc. 2. 14. Vrede ſy op aerden ; Iohan. 14.27. Vrede laet ick u : mynen Vrede geve ick u ; Rom. 10.15. en Eſai. 52.7 : Hoe lieffelijck zijn de voeten vanden genen die den Vrede ende dat goet verkondigē; Pſal.133. Siet hoe fijn en hoe lieffelijc iſt , dat Broe-

Broederen in eendracht by malkanderen woonen : 't is gelyck als eenen koſtelycken Balſem, die daer vandē Hoofde Aarons neder vloeyt in zynen gheheelen Baerdt , ende neder vloeyt tot in zijn Kleet: gelijck den Dauwe die van Hermon af valt op de Bergen Syons : Want aldaer belooft den Heere den zeghen en dat Leven altoos eñ eeuwelijck; Rom. 12. 18. hebt Vrede met alle Menſchen, ſo vele als in u is; Rom. 14. 17 het Rijcke Godts en is noch ſpyſe noch dranck , maer gerechticheydt en vrede, en blijtſchap inden Heyligen Gheeſt; verſ. 9. daeromme laet ons volgen dat tot Vrede ende beteringhe onder malkanderen dient ; 1. Corinth. 7. 15. Godt heeft ons in Vrede geroepen ; 2. Corinth. 13. 11. ten laetſten myne Broeders, verblijt u ; weeſt volkomen ; trooſt u ; hebt eenderley moet ; weeſt vreedſaem, ſoo ſal Godt der Liefden ende des

(§ 3)   Vie-

Vredes met u zyn. Defe ende meer andere Schriftuerplaetfen tot onfer leeringe ter herten nemende, ende in de vreefe Gods overlegghende, en bevindende dat wy daerin gemift hebben, eñ daer door van den wegh des Vreedts afghedwaelt zynde, eñ onfe wegen met David Pfal. 119.59. befinnende, hevet ons hoogh-tijdt ghedacht, met David onfe voeten tot des Heeren getuygenis te keerē, ons voor Godt ende onfen Naeften te verootmoedigen: feggende cla-ge Ierem. 3.42: Wy, wy hebben ge-fondight, eñ zyn ongehoorfaem ge-weeft, daeromme en hebt ghy ons niet gefpaert, onfe gemoederē hier door ontfteken, eñ onfe herten met Lydia (Act. 16. 14.) geopent zynde, hebben wy den aenghenamen tydt waergenomē, en met de verftroyde Schapen (waer van wy gheen van de minfte waren)die met ons in een ge-loove, leeringe en belevinghe ftaen ende

ende wandelen, den vervallen Vre-de wederomme voor-ghenomen op te rechten, ende alfo in Liefde ende Vrede met elkander te leven en te wandelen, tot groot-makinge vandē hoogwaerdigen ende heyligen Na-me Godts: tot bouwinge ende be-teringe ons felfs, en tot ftichtinghe van onfen Naeften, eyndelinge tot onfer alder zielen Salicheydt: waer toe den bermhertighen Godt (die een Godt des Vreedes ende niet des twifts ende tweedrachts en is) door zynen ghebenedyden Soone, onfen Heer eñ Salichmaker Iefū Chriftū, fonder den welcken wy niet en ver-mogen, Iohan. 15.5. zynen genadi-gen zegen wil geven, Amen.

Wy hebben om oorfaeck (in 't be-gin van defe Voor-reden aen ghe-trocken) niet konnen naelaten, alle ware Liet hebbers des Vreeds mede te deylen: en mitfdefen kennelijck te maken de hoedanicheyt, ende op **wat**

Voor-reden.

wat Articulen des Geloofs (dē Vrede tot Dordrecht by ons in den Iare
1 6 3 2. den 21. April wederomme
vernieuwt , ende door een volkomē
vergevinge, loflatinghe ende quijt-
fcheldinge vā alle voorgaende ver-
grijpinge, miſ handelinge en bindin-
ge aen weder-zyden gheſchiet) wederomme opgerecht eñ beveſticht
is : op dat niemandt na deſen, door
onkunde, ſoude laſterē het gene dat
fy niet en weten. Gebruyckt dit na-
volghende dan tot uwen beſten , en
vaert wel.

In Haerlem deſen 8. April, door
een Liefhebber des Vreeds.

Wy

Y Bzoederē/met onſen
Oudtſten ende Diena-
ren (onwaerdigh) der
vereenighde Gemeente
Godts al-hier te Dor-
dzecht : Als oock wy ondergheſchze-
ben Oudtſten/Dienaren ende Bzoe-
ders/ die als Mede-hulpers al-hier
ontboden/gheſonden/ghekomen/ en
elcks ſoo booz ons ſelven / ende van
wegen onſe Ghemepnte/ in des Heeren Name al-hier inder Ghemepnte
vergadert / ende met haer vereenight
zijn: Wenſchen t'ſamen aen alle Ge-
mepnten/Mede-hulperen/Bzoeders
ende Medegenoten des algemepnen
Chziſtelijcken Gheloofs/in alle Ste-
den eñ Plaetſen daer deſe onſe openbare ende generale Bzoederlicke ver-

A   eenni=

eeninghe / Bebzedinghe ende Ver-
dzagh kennelijck ghemaeckt oft ver-
toont sal wozden/ van den Almachti-
ghen/ Eenighen/ Eeuwighen/ On-
begrijpelijcken Godt / Hemelsche
Wijsheydt / ende Goddelijcke Verlichtinghe / om daer dooz te moghen
pzoeven / onderschepden ende naer-
volghen 't ghene dat tot uwer ende
onser alderbeste Vzede ende Beteringhe onder malkanderen noodigh/
vooz Gode behaeghlijck / ende vooz
de menschen ghevalligh is / om alsoo
te wandelen ghelijck als uwen ende
onsen roep betaemt: op dat wy met
V. L. ende ghy met ons hier nae-
maels/ nesfens alle Vzoome uptver-
koozen Godts Heylighen ende Be-
minden / dooz onsen Heere Jesum
Chzistum / eeuwigh saligh ende be-
houden moghen wozden : Daer toe
de goede ende getrouwe Godt V.L.
en ons wil helpen/ sijnen ghenadigen
zegen verleenen/ en al te samen waerdigh ende bequaem maken / Amen.

Vooz

3

Voozder dient desen : Alsoo kennelijck ende openbaer is/ watter vooz
desen ende over langhe jaren herre-
waerts/ in vele ofte sommighe plaetsen / ende dat om verschepden saec-
ken/ al dzoevighe onrust/ verwerrin-
ghe ende verstropinghe / jae separa-
tie / scheuringhe ende deplinghe onder de eens-gheloofs-ghenooten ontstaen ende ghebolght is/ ende dat onder alle de selve geensins daer van de
minste en zp / de ghene die over eenighe jaeren dooz den Twist van den
Huys-koop/ met het ghebolgh ende
aenkleben van dien/ in der Gemeynte tot Franeker/ als mede in deel andere plaetsen ontstaen ende gheballen
is / tot groote lasteringhe van den
waerdighen Name Gods/ on-eere/
smaedt ende verachtinge zynder Ge-
meynte/ als oock de menichvuldighe
quetsinge/ aenstoot ende arghernisse
die daer beroozsaeckt/ ghegheben ende ghenomen is: soo datmen sulcks
met hertelijck berouw ende leedtwe-

A 2   sen

sen wel magh beklaeghen/ende wen=
schen dat het selve nopt ghetweest ofte
gheschiedt en waere. Maer ghelpck
de fauten van vele zaecken ghemep=
nelijck beter van achteren als van
vooren ghesien ende onderscheyden
konnen wozdt: even alsoo is 't oock
in deser saecke/ want hoemen de selve
met onpartydigher herten langher
overleght/ wel doozstet/ ende naer=
denckt/ watter al quade bzuchtē upt
sulcke ende dier-ghelijcke Twisten
voozt-ghekomen zijn/ hoemen in 't
gemoedt meer ende meer gewis ende
seeckerder wozdt/ dat de schuldt ende
oozsaecke van dien/ niet gheheelaen
eender zijde/ maer dat aen weder-sij=
den grootelijckr ghemist ende versien
is; ende datmen in het straffen/ af=
sonderen/ ende verwerpen van mal=
kanderen/ al te pverich ende onma=
tich heeft ghehandelt.

Want overmits dat het aē de pzin=
cipale Leverep ende Ken-tepcken der
ware Navolghers Chzisti/ over we=
der=

der-zijden te veel ontbzoocken heeft/
namelijck aen de Liefde/ die daer is   Joä 13.35
de Hooft-somme ende 't alder-groot=   Colo.2.14
ste Ghebodt/ de vervullinghe van al=
le Wetten/ jae den bandt der volko=
menheydt/daer dooz de eens-geloofs
ghenooten aen den Heere/ ende daer
beneffens als een herte ende ziele/ in
Vzede ende Eendzacht aen malkan=
deren/als leden eens lichaems/so hoo=
ghe verbonden zijn/om daer dooz al=
toos ende alder-weghen malkande=
ren te voozkomen/verdzaeghen ende
verghenen/ de zonden/ ghebzeecken   Luc.6.36.
ende feplen des Naesten te bedecken/
medē-lyden hebben/ barmhertichept
bewijsen/ ende sachtelijck met mal=   2Coz.5.11
kanderen omme te gaen/om het ghe=   Eze.34.4.
quetste niet voozder te bzeecken/noch
het zwacke te verstooten oft onder te
dzucken / maer andersins altoos een   Phil.2.3.
ander hoogher als hem selven te ach=
ten/om alsoo de oneerlijckste leden die   1Co.12.23
ons qualijckst aenstaē/ wat toe/ ende
de selve de meeste eere te gheven/ daer
              A 3   dooz

dooz veel ongheluck/ twist ende twee=
dzacht kan boozkomen wozden.

   Maer desen waerdigen bandt der
Liefden verkoelt/ verswackt/ oft by
vele ghenoechsaem gebzoken zijnde/
soo isser in plaetse van dien (upt dat

mat. 13.25

quade zaedt dooz den vpandt in veel
slaeperige menschen haren acker des
herten ghewozpen) soo een bitteren

Heb. 12.15

woztel ghegroept ende ghewassen/
daer dooz alle erreur/ verwerringhe/
en quade vzuchten/ als haet/ nijdt/
twist/ tweedzacht/ bpten/ verstin=
den/ scheuren en bernen upt booz=
ghekomen ende gheopenbaert zijn:
Ende ghelijck als upt een klepne
voncke (wanneerse aen-gheblasen
ofte niet by tijts ghebluscht en wozt)
dickmaels eene groote verteeringhe
volght/ even alsoo is 't oock in deser
saecke ghegaen; Soo datmen wel
metter waerhepdt segghen mach/ dat
niet alleen den Huys-koop/ noch
oock 't ghevolgh en aenkleven van
dien/ maer dat veel eer de wederzijdse
Son=

7

Sonden/ de oozsaecke daer van wel
mach ende behoozt toegheepghent te
wozden.

   Alle 't welcke wy niet alleene hier
tot Dozdzecht/ maer oock in vele an=
dere plaetsen hoe langs hoe meer ter
herten ghenomen/ ende 't selve over=
lept ende nae-ghedacht hebben; als
mede daer beneffens/ dat ons so veel
hooghwaerdige en treffelijcke Vooz=
beelden en Exempelen der Oudtva=
ders in de Heplighe Schzift/ tot lee=
ringhe ende aenwijsinghe naeghela=
ten ende booz ooghen gestelt zijn/ op
dat wy daer in/ als in eenen Spiegel/
sonden sien ende aenmercken/ hoe de
rechte eens-gheloofs-ghenooten met
malkanderen in begane/ ghepasseer=
de ende teghenwoozdighe saken van
verschil/ twist ende onrust/ behoozen
te doen/ te handelen/ ende te arbep=
den/ om malkanderen wederom met
eerbiedinghe te boozkomen/ onder=
scheppen ende te moete gaen: ghe=
lijck als wy bevinden dat de Patri=
A 4   archen

archen ende Propheten met veel vzo=
me/jae d'Apostelen als Herders/Va=
ders en Voozgangers der Gemeyn=
te/ selfs ghedaen / en der gheloobighe
Chzistenen alles soo hooghe belast en
Heb. 13.20 bevolen hebben/om hare nabolghers
Cant. 1.6. te zijn/ghelijck als sy selber den groo=
den Herder/ zyne exempelen/ voet=
stappen/ leere ende leben nagebolght
hebben: op dat/ soo doende/ het twi=
sten/ kyben/ byten/ verslinden/ quet=
sen/ verderven/ scheurē en bernen een=
mael mochte op-houden / ende dat
men in plaetse van dien/ met goeder=
Psa. 85.11 tierenheydt en trouwe/ jae in Liefde
mat. 18.12 en Vzede malkanderē mochten ont=
moeten: om het verlozen te soecken/
Eze. 34.16 het verstropde ende verdwaelde we=
derom by-een te versamelen/ het ghe=
Esa. 58.12 quetste te verbinden/ het verballene
te repareren en op te rechten/ ja de re=
Esa. 57.12 ten te vertuynen/ de heubelen te slech=
ten / de steenen des aenstoots wech te
ruymen/ de weghen te beteren / ende
alsoo een effen bane te maecken / dat
oock

oock de onwetende daer op niet en
mochten doolen/ maer altoos en al=
der weghen alsoo nae-bolghen wat
vooz Godt behaechlijck/ ende tot der
Ghemeynten beste / vzede ende bete=
ringe onder malkanderen meest van
nooden is.

Over sulckx soo hebben wy onder
den onsen te weder-ziiden/ naer vooz
gaende ernstelijcke Ghebeden tot
Godt / van langher-handt ghear=
beydt/ om 't ghene inde ghepasseerde
saecke / soo in ende naer den Twist
van den Huys-koop/ onder ons ende
den onsen gevallen/ ende tot noch tos
gheschiedt is/ alle 't selbe bolghens de
exempelen der Ouden / ende nae de
leeringhe der heyligher Schzistuere/
wederom wech te nemen / ende om
tot Vzede/ Reparatie/ Versoeninghe
ende Vereeniginghe met malkande=
ren te moghen komen / ende is eyn=
delijck dooz des Heeren ghenade en=
de Goddelijcke hulpe / de saecke soo
verre ghebzacht/ dat wy ghesament=
A 5.   lijck

lijck ter weder-zyden / soo wel d'een als d'ander / van veel ende verschey-den plaetsen / al-hier tot Dordrecht verschreven / ontbodé / ende oock dier oorsaken vergadert ende by den an-deren ghekomen zijn.

Ende also ter weder-zyden in des Heeren Name te samen by-een met den anderen vergadert zijnde: Soo is doen by ons onwaerdighe / met malkanderen in minne ende vriendt-schap/ soo verre met goede bequaem-heydt / inde vreese Gods/ versproken ende overleydt / dat wy ons daer nae met bidden ende smeecken tot den Heere hebben begheven / de welcke door zynen ghenadighen zegen / on-ser alder weder-zijds herte alsoo be-rept ende tot malcanderen geneyght heeft / daer van hem gebedijdt alleen lof en danck zy / dat wy na hertelicke Schuldt-bekenteniße / aengaende de voornoemde saecke / ontbonden / vry en los ghelaten hebben: ghelijck wy oock vry en los laeten / ende ontbin-den

Esai. 58.6

den mitsdesen alle den genen / die wy ende onse voorighe Voorganghers/ ende der selver Gemeynten voor de-sen / dier saecken halven / ghebonden/ ghestraft afghesondert / ofte erghens anders mede beswaert hebben.

Ende boven dien / soo hebben wy met hertelijck berouw en leedtwesen malkanderen om vergiffenisse gebe-den/ ende dier volghens oock ter we-der-zyden/ elckx den anderen uyt op-rechter herten / alles volkomelijcken bergheven ende quijtghescholden/ ge-lijck of 't nopt gheschiedt en waere; als wy oock vergheven ende quijt-schelden midtsdesen/ alle 't ghene wat by ons ofte onse voorighe Voorgan-ghers ende der selver Ghemeynten/ soo in 't generael als particulier/ aen-gaende de sake van den Huys-koop tot Franeker/ met den aenkleven eñ ende ghevolgh van dien / het zy met woorden/ wercken/ boecken/ brieven/ of 't ghene in eenigherley andere ma-niere (niet uytghesondert) versuymt/ ver-

verschuldicht en mishandelt is/ende
daer wp malkanderen ofte pemandt
van den onsen ter weder-zpden/ de
eene den anderen tot deser tijdt toe/
mede bedroeft/ ghequetst ofte ghear=
ghert souden moghen hebben.

Over sulcks soo hebben wp oock
ghelijckelijck/alle/ende te samen met
malkanderen/ onsen Ghenadighen/
Barmhertighen Godt ende Hemel=
schen Vader/ in den Name van zp=
nen lieben Soone onsen Heere Je=

Mat.6.12 sum Christum/ ernstelijck met her=
telijck berouw en leedtwesen/ ende
upt oprechter hertelijcker mepninge/

Spz. 28,8 ende van repnder herten ghebeden
ende ghesmeeckt/ om quijtschelding=
ghe ende volkomen verghevinghe
van alles watter tot hier toe bp ons
ende den onsen ter weder-zpden in
deser saecke/ oft anders in eenigerlep
manieren/ teghens spne hooge Ma=
jestept/en tegen malkanderen/oft te=
ghen eenich mensche ter wereldt ver=
supmt en verschuldigt mochte wesen.
Ende

13

Ende tot bewijs en bevestinghe
van een oprecht ende volkomen ver=
dzagh/versoeninghe ende vereeninge
met malcanderen/soo hebben wp ter
weder-zpden/ metter handt ende den
lieffelicken Kus des Vredes malcan=
deren ontfanghen/ende elcks den an=
deren aenghenomen/ in den Name
des Heeren/ gelpck ende als den genē
betaemt/ die in eene ghemepnschap
met hem ende onder malkanderen
staen ende vereenight zijn.

Onder welcke dese onse Veree=
ninghe/ wp mede begrepen ende
verbanghen hebben/ alle absente/
generaele ende particuliere Mede=
ghenooten/ in haere ofte onse plaet=
sen woonachtich/ soo wel die ontbo=
den zijn gheweest als oock alle ande=
re/ niemandt uptghesondert. Ghe=
lijck als wp oock de selve hier in be=
grijpen/ verbanghen/ ende tot ons=
waerdts benoodighen midts-desen:
als mede alle Gheloofs-ghenooten/
die met ons eenderlep in gelijcke goe=
de Wille/

be Wille/ Gheloobe/ Leeringhe/ ende
Belebinghe staen/ofte naemaels met
ons mede souden moghen bolghen/
om boortaen met malkanderen/ ter
eeren Gods/ en stichtinghe/ bouwin=
ghe/ende beteringhe der Ghemeynte
onder den anderen/als een herte ende
een ziele/ vreedsamelijck te leben ende
te wandelen/ in voeghen gelijck boor
desen/ ende als onsen roep betaemt/
bolghens ons al-ghemeyne Chri=
stelijcke Gheloobe/waer ban de prin=
cipaelste Artijckelen upt den Woor=
de Gods/ in 't korte hier nabolgende
gestelt ende bpghevoeght zijn.

Acto?.4.12

Voorstellinghe van de principale
Articulen onses al-gemeynē Christelijcken Gheloofs, gelijck de selve in onse Ghemeynte doorgaens
gheleert ende beleeft vvorden.

T En eersten: Naedien wp be=
tupght vinden/ dat het zonder
Gheloobe onmoghelijck is Godt te
behae=

Hebr.11.6

behaeghen; ende wie tot Godt ko=
men wil/ die moet ghelooben datter
een Godt is/ ende dat hp een betael=
der zijn sal den ghenen die hem soec=
ken. Over sulcks soo belpden wp
met den monde/ende ghelooben met=
ter herten/beneffens alle Vroome/na
der hepligher Schriftupre/ in een ee=
nen eeuwigē/ Almachtigen eñ onbe=
grijpelijcken Godt/ Vader ende So=
ne ende H.Geest/ en geen meer/ noch
gheen ander: boor den welcken oock
gheen Godt ghemaeckt of gheweest
en is/noch oock naer hem niet zijn en
sal: Want upt hem/ door hem/ ende
in hem zijn alle dinghen: Hem zp lof/
prijs ende eere/ van eeuwichepdt tot
eeuwichepdt/Amen.

Deut.6.4.
Gen. 17.1
Esai.46.8
Ioa.5.7.

Ro.11.36.

Desen selven eenighen Godt/ die
daer werckt alle dinck in alles/ die
ghelooben ende belpden wp/ dat een
Schepper is van alle sienelijcke ende
onsienelijcke dinghen; dewelcke bin=
nen ses daghen Hemel ende Aerde/
de Zee ende alles watter in is/ ghe=
schapen/

1Cor.12.6

Genes.1.*

Act. 14.14

schapen/ghemaeckt ende toeberepdt
heeft : ende dat hp de selve ende alle
spne wercken noch regeert ende on-
derhoudt / dooz sijne Wijshept/ Mo-
ghenthepdt / ende dooz den woozde
sijnder kracht.

Ende als hp sijne wercken vol-
bzacht / ende nae sijn wel-behaeghen
goet ende opzecht/elcks in sijn natue-
re/wesen ende epghenschap gheozdi-
neert ende berepdt hadde/ Soo heeft
hp daer beneffens oock den eersten
Gen. 1.27 Mensche/ onser alder Bader Adam/
gheschapen/ ende hem een Lichaem
Genes. 2.7 ghegheven/d'welck hp upt den Aer-
den-klomp ghemaeckt/ende hem een
levendighen adem in sijn Neuse ghe-
blasen heeft/ also dat hp ghewozden
Genes. 5.1 is een levende ziele van Godt/nae sp-
nen Beelde ende Gelijckenisse/in op-
rechter gherechtichepdt ende heplig-
hepdt / tot den Eeuwighen Leven
gheschapen : Ende heeft hem boven
alle andere Creatueren sonderlinghe
aenghesien/ ende met vele hooghe ende
heerlijcke

heerlijcke gaben verciert/inden Lust-
hoff ofte Paradijse ghestelt / ghebodt **Gen. 2.18**
ende verbodt ghegheven : ende heeft **Gen. 2.17**
oock daer nae van den selven Adam/
een Ribbe ghenomen/ ende een Wijff **Gen. 2.22**
daer upt gebouwt/tot hem gebzacht/
ende de selve hem tot een Hulpe / Ge-
sellinne ende Hups-bzouwe toe-ghe-
voeght ende ghegheven : ende heeft
dien volghens oock ghemaeckt / dat
van desen eenighen eersten Mensche **Act. 17.26**
Adam/ alle menschen op het ghehee-
le Aerdtrijck woonende/ gegenereert
ende voortghekomen zijn.

Ten tweeden / Ghelooven ende belpden wp / naer in-houdt der
Hepligher Schriftuere : dat de selve
onser alder eerste Voor-ouderen / A-
dam ende Eva / in desen heerelijcken
standt / daerse in gheschapen waren/
niet langhe en zijn ghebleven / maer
de selve / dooz de listichepdt ende be- **Genes. 3.6**
dzogh der Slanghen ende npdichept
des Dupvels / verboert ende verlepdt
zijnde/soo hebben sp dat hooghe ghe-
B   bodt

bodt Gods overghetreden/ ende zijn
haren Schepper ongehoorsaem ge-
woorden: door welcke ongehoorsaem-
heydt de Sonde in de Werelds ghekomen is/ende door de sonde de doot/
ende is also doorgedrongen over alle
menschen/ aenghesien sp alle ghesou-
dight hebben/ ende over sulcks den
toorn Gods ende verdoemenisse op
haer ghelaen/ daerom sp van Godt
upt den Paradijse ofte Lusthof ghe-
dreven zijn/ om het Aerdrijck te bou-
wen/met commer haer daer op te ge-
neeren/ ende in 't sweet des aensichts
haer broodt te eten / tot dat sp weder
tot Aerde souden worden/daerse van
ghenomen waren: Ende dat sp over
sulcks door de selve eenighe Sonde/
soo gheheel verre vervallen/afghewe-
ken/ en van Godt verbreemt zijn ge-
worden / soo datse noch door haer sel-
ven/noch door niemandt haerder na-
komelingen / noch door Engelen oft
Menschen/ noch door gheen ander
Creatuere indē Hemel noch opAerdē
weder-

Esdr.3.7

Rom. 5.12
en vers.18

Gen. 3.23

Psal. 49.8

Apoc. 5.*

wederom opgheholpen/ verlost/ ofte
met God versoent en konden wordē/
maer datse eeuwelijck verloren had-
den moeten blpven ligghen/ ten ware dat Godt (die hem over sijn schep-
sel wederom ontfermde) daer in ghe-
sien/ ende met sijn Liefde en Barm-
herticheydt daer tusschen ghekomen
ware.

Ten derden : Aengaende de Op-
rechtinghe des eersten mensche ende
sijne nakomelinghen/ daer van help-
den ende ghelooven wp/ niet teghen-
staende desen haren val/ overtredin-
ghe ende zonde/ ende hoewel bp haer
gantsch gheen vermoghen en was/
dat Godt daerom noch even wel haer
niet en heeft willen gheheelijcken ver-
werpen/ noch eeuwelijck verloren laten blpven/maer dat hp haer wederom tot hem gheroepen/ vertroost ende getoont heeft/ datter bp hem noch
middel haerder versoeninghe was/
namelijck dat onbevlechte Lam (ofte
Sone) Gods/ die daer tot al voor des

Ioa.3.16.

Ioa.1.29.

B 2 　　We-

1 Pet. 1.19
Gen. 3.15
1 Joa. 3.8
1. Joa. 2.1

Werelts beginsel voorsien/ ende haer noch inde Paradijse sijnde/ tot troost/ verlossinghe ende salicheydt/ soo voor haer en alle hare nakomelinghen belooft en toeghesepdt/ ja haer door het gheloove van doen aen/ als epghen ghegheven en gheschoncken is/ daer alle vroome Oudt-vaderen die de-

Heb. 11.13
en hf. 39.

se belofte menich-mael is vernieuwt/ nae verlanght/ ondersocht/ ende door het Gheloove van verre te ghemoete

Gal. 4.4.

ghesien/ en op de vervullinghe verwacht hebben/ dat hy komende/ 't gevallen menschelijcke gheslachte van haere zonden/ schult en ongerechtigheydt/ wederom verlossen/ vry maecken ende op-helpen soude.

Ten vierden/ soo ghelooven ende belyden wy voorder: Dat/ als desen tijdt der beloften/ daer alle vroome Oudtvaderen soo seer nae verlangt/ en op ghewacht hebben/ omghekomen en vervult was/ dat doenmaels

Joa. 4.25.
joa. 16.28.

desen voor-belooften Messias/Verlosser en Salichmaecker/ van Godt uyt-

uptgegaen/ gesonden/ ende (na voorsegginghe der Propheten/ en het getuyghenisse der Euangelisten) in de werelt/ jae in't vleesch gekomen/ geopenbaert/ en 't Woordt selfs Vleesch ende Mensch ghewoorden is/ ende dat hy in de Maghet Maria (die onder-troudt was met eenen Man/ ghenaemt Joseph/ van Davids Huys) is ontfanghen/ ende dat sy dien als haren eersten ghebooren Soone tot Bethlehem ghebaert/in doecken gewonde en in een Kribbe gelept heeft.

1. tim. 3.15
Joa. 1.14.
Mat. 1.22
Luc. 2.7.
en hf. 21,

Wy belyden en ghelooven oock: Dat dit de selfde is/ wiens uptganck van aenbegin ende van eeuwighept gheweest is/ sonder begin der daghen of epnde des levens: Die selfs de A/ ende O/ begin en epnde/ de eerste/ en de laetste betupght woordt te zijn: en dat desen oock de selfde is/ en gheen ander/die voorsien/ belooft/ gesonden ende in de werelt ghekomen is/ ende die Godts eenighen/ eersten ende epghen Sone is/ die voor Johannes

Mich. 5.1
Hebr. 7.3.
Apoc. 1.8.
en vers. 18.
Joa. 3.16.
Hebr. 1.6.
rom. 8.32.
Joa. 1. 30.

B 3   de

de Dooper / voor Abraham / voor de
Wereldt / jae Davids Heere en alder
wereldt Godt is / de eerste ghebooren voor al Creatueren / die in de werelt gebracht ende hem een Lichaem
berept is / dat hy selfs overghegeven
heeft tot een offer ende gaeve / Godt
tot eenen soeten Reuck / jae tot troost /
verlossinghe ende salicheydt van alle /
en 't gheheele menschelijcke ghellachte.

Maer aengaende hoe en op wat
wyse dit waerdige Lichaem berept /
ende hoe dat het Woordt Vleesch / eñ
hy selfs Mensche ghewozden is / daer
aen vernoeghen wy ons met de verklaringhe / die de waerdighe Euangelisten in haere beschrijvinghe daer
van ghedaen ende naeghelaten hebben / nae de welcke wy hem met alle
Heyligen / belyden ende bekennen te
wesen den Sone van den Levendigen Godt / daer alle onse hope / troost /
verlossinghe ende salighepdt in bestaet / ende dat wy de selve oock in
niemant

Margin references (left):
Mt. 22. 41
Col. 1. 15.
Hebr. 10. 5
Luc. 1. 30. 31.
Joa. 20. 30 31.
Mt 16. 16

niemant anders / mogen noch en behoozen te soecken.

Voorder ghelooven ende belyden
wy met der Schriftuere : Nae dat
hy hier zynen loop voleydt ende het
werck / daerom hy ghesonden ende in
de werelt ghekomen was / volbracht
hadde / dat hy nae de voorsienighepet
Godts / is overgelevert in de handen
der ongherechtiger / ende dat hy onder den Rechter Pontio Pilato gheleden heeft / ende dat hy ghekruyst /
ghestorven / begraven / ten derden dage wederom vander doodt verresen /
ende ten Hemel opghevaren is : ende
dat hy sit ter rechter hant Godts der
Majestept in den hooghsten / en van
daer wederom komen sal om te oordeelen de levende ende de doode.

Ende dat alsoo den Sone Godts
gestorven is / ende voor allen den doot
ghesmaeckt ende sijn dierbare bloedt
vergoten heeft : Ende dat hy daer
door de Slanghe den kop vertreden /
de wercken des Duyvels gebroken /

B 4 het

Margin references (right):
Lu. 22. 53
Luc. 23. 1.
Luc. 24. 5. ende 6.
Lu. 24. 50
Gen. 3. 15
1. Joa. 3. 8

24

Col.2. 14. het hantschrift te niete gedaé/ eñ vergiffenisse der zonden voor 't gheheele
menschelijcke gheslachte verworven
Rom.5.18 heeft: Eñ dat hy also een oorsake der
eewiger salichept gewozden is / voor
alle den ghenen (van Adam aen / tot
aen 't epnde des Weereldts) die elckx
in zynen tijdt aen hem ghelooven ende gehoorsaem zijn.

Ten vijfden/ ghelooven ende belpden wy oock : Dat hy voor sijn
Jer. 31.31 Hemelvaert sijn nieuwe Testament
opgherecht/ ingheftelt/ ende naedien
het een eeuwich Testament zijn ende
blpven soude / dat hy 't selve met zp-
Hebz.9.15 nen dierbaren Bloede bevesticht en-
16. 17. de bezeghelt / den zynen ghegheven
Mt.26.27 ende naeghelaten/ jae soo hooghe belaft ende bevolen heeft / en dat het sel-
Galat.1.8 ve noch door Engel/ noch door men-
1 Tim.6.3 schen verandert / noch af of toeghe-
daen en mach wozden : ende dat hy
dat selve / als daer in begrepen zijnde
Joa.15.15 den gheheelen vollen Raedt en wille
zijns Hemelschen Vaders (voor soo
veel

veel ter salichept van noode is) door
zijn liebe Apostelen / Zepnd-boden
ende Dienaers / die hy daer toe be- Mt.28.19
roepen/ verkoozen ende in alle de we- Mr.16.13
reldt ghesonden heeft/ende onder alle
Volcken/ Natien ende Tonghen/ in Lu.24.45
zynen Naem laeten verkondighen/ ende 46.
predicken en ghetupghen boete ende
berghevinghe der zonden / ende dat
hy dien volghens daer in alle menschen sonder onderschepdt / voor soo
vele alsser den inhoudt van dien door
het Gheloove/als ghehoorsame Kin-
deren/sonden naerkomen/achtervol-
ghen en beleven/ voor sijne Kinderen Rom.8.17
ende wettighe Erfghenaemen heeft
doen verklaeren : Alsoo dat hy van
die weerdighe erffenisse der eeuwiger
Salichept / niemandt gesecludeert
noch uptghesloten heeft / anders als
alleen die ongheloovighe en onghe-
hoorsame/hertneckighe of onbekeer-
lijcke menschen / die 't selve verach- Act. 13.46
ten / ende door haer epghen selfs be-
gane sonden verschuldigen/ende haer
B 5 daer

daer toe alfoo des eeuwighen levens
onwaerdigh maken.

Ten feften gelooven ende belpden
wp : Naedemael het opfet des men-
Gen.8.21 fchen herte boos is van der jeught
aen / ende derhalven tot alle onghe-
rechticheydt / zonde ende booshepdt
gheneghen is / dat over fulcks de eer-
fte Leffe van 't weerdighe Nieuwe
Teftament des Soons Godts / is
Mar.1.15 boete en beteringhe des levens / ende
Eze.12.1 dat daerom de menfchen oozen hebben om te hoozen / en herten om te
verftaen / opzechte vzuchten van boete moeten doen / haer leven beteren /
Mar.1.15 den Euangelium gelooven / het quade laten / het goede doen / ophouden
van onrecht / ende aflaeten van zon-
Colof.3.9
en 10.
Ephef.4.
21. en 22. den / den ouden Menfche met zpne
wercken upt-trecken ende den nieuwen aen-doen / die nae Godt gefcha-
pen is in oprechter gerechtigheyt eñ
heplighept : Want noch Doopfel /
Avondtmael / Ghemepnte / noch eenighe andere uptwendighe Cermo-
nien /

nien / fonder Gheloove ende Weder-
gheboozte / veranderinghe ofte ver-
nieuwinghe des levens / niet en mach
helpen om Godt te behagen / ofte om
eenighen trooft of belofte der Salig-
hept van hem te mogen verwerven :
Maer men moet met waerachtiger Heb.10.21
en 22.
herten / en in volkomen gheloove tot
Godt gaen / ende in Jefum Chzi- Joa.7.38.
ftum gelooven / gelijck als de Schzift
fept ende van hem ghetupght / dooz
welcken Gheloove men vergiffeniffe
der zonden verkrijght / gheheplicht /
gerechtveerdicht eñ Kinderen Godts
jae fijn Ghefinthepdt / Natuere ende
Wefen deelachtich wozt / als die dooz
dat onverganckelijcke zaedt / van boven nieuw upt Godt / wedergheboo-
ren zijn.

Ten fevenden / aengaende het
Doopfel / daer van belpden ende bekennen wp : Dat alle Boetveerdi- Act.2.38.
ghe Gheloovighe / die dooz 't Gheloove / Weder-gheboozte / ende Ver-
nieuwinghe des Heplighen Gheefts
met

met Godt vereenicht ende inden Hemel aengheschzeven zijn : Op soo-
danighen Schziftmatigen belpdin-
ghe des Gheloofs ende vernieuwin-
ghe des Levens / nae het bevel Chzi-
sti / ende Leeringhe / Erempel ende
Ghebzupck der Apostelen / behoozen
Mt 28.20 in dien hoogh-weerdigen Name des
Vaders / ende des Soons / ende des
Hepligen Gheests / tot begrabin-
ghe haerder Sonden met water ge-
doopt / ende alsoo inde Gemepnschap
Mt 28.20 der Hepligen inghelijft te wozden /
Rom.6.4. om dan voozts te leeren onderhou-
Mt 16.15 den alle / dat den Sone Godts den
Mat 3.15 sijnen gheleert / nagelaten ende bevo-
Act.2. 28. len heeft.
Act. 8. 11.
Act. 9.18.
ende 10.47
ende 16.33
Col.2. 11.
12.

Ten achtsten / soo ghelooben ende
belpden wp : Een sichtbare Ghemepnte Godts / namelijck / die alsoo
als voozen verhaelt / opzechte boete
1 Coz.12.* doen / recht ghelooben en recht ghe-
doopt zijn / met Godt in den Hemel
vereenight / ende in de Gemepnschap
der Hepligen hier op Aerden recht
zijn

zijn inghelijfc / de selve bekennen wp
te wesen dat uptverkozen Ghellach- 1 Pet. 2. 4
te / dat Conincklijcke Pziesterdom /
het Heplighe Volck / de welcke betupght wozden Chzisti Bzupdt en Joa.3.29.
Hupsbzouwe / ja kinderen ende Erf- Apoc.19.7
ghenamen des Eeuwighen Levens Tit. 3.6.7
te zijn / een Hutte / Tabernakel ende
Woon-stadt Godts in den Gheest / Eph.2.19
ghetimmert op der grondt der Apo- 20.21.
stelen en Pzopheten / daer van Chzi-
stus selfs den Hoecksteen (waer op mat.16.18
sijn Vergaderinge gesticht is) wozdt
betupght te wesen. Dese Gemepn-
te des Lebendighen Godts / die hp 1 Pet.1.18
dooz sijn epgen dierbare Bloedt ver- 19.
wozden / ghekocht ende verlost heeft /
ende daer hp volghens sijn Belofte /
tot troost en beschermynghe alle da- mat.28.20
ghe tot der Wereldt epnde / bp sijn
ende bipben / jae onder woonen ende 2 Coz.6.16.
wandelen sal / ende haer bewaren dat
ghen stroomen noch plas-regenen / Mat 7.25
jae selfs de Poozten der Hellen / haer mat.16.18
niet en sullen beweghen of oberwel-
dighen:

dighen : De felve mach men bekennen aen het Schriftmaetich Ghe-
loove/ Leere/ Liefde/ en Godtfalighe
wandelinge : als oock aende vrucht-
bare Belevinghe/ Ghebruyck ende
Onderhoudinghe van de ware Ordinantien Chrifti/ de welcke hy den
fynen foo hooghe belaft ende bevolen
heeft.

Ten neghenden / aengaende de
Dienften ende Verkiefinghe in der
Ghemeynte/daer van ghelooven ende belyden wy : Alfoo de Gemeynte fonder Dienft en Ordinantie / in
wafdom niet en kan beftaen/ noch in
bouwinghe blyven/ dat over fulcks
de Heere Chriftus felfs(als een huys-
Eph. 4.10 vader in fijn Huys) fijn Dienften
11.12. ende Ordinantien inghestelt/ gheor-
dineert/ belaft en bevolen heeft/ hoe
een yeghelijck daer in wandelen/fijn
werck en beroepinghe waer nemen
ende doen fal nae behooren/ ghelpyck
1Pet.2.29 hy felve als den ghetrouwen groo-
ten Overften Herder/ende Biffchop
onfer

onfer Zielen/ daerom gefonden ende
in de Werelde ghekomen is : Niet **mat.12.19**
om te quetfen/ te breecken / oft om de
Zielen der menfchen te verderven : **mat.18.11**
maer om te heelen ende te ghenefen/
het verloozen te foecken / den thuyn **Eph.2.13**
ende middel-wandt af te breecken/
om van twee / een te maecken/ ende
alfoo uyt Joden/ Heydenen en alle **Gal.3.28.**
Geflachten een Kudde tot eene ghe-
meynfchap in fynen Name te verfa-
melen/daer hy felve (op dat niemant
dwalende of verlozen foude gaen)fijn
Leven voor ghelaten/ ende haer ter **Joa.10.9/**
11.15. Salighepdt alfoo ghedient/ vry ghemaeckt ende verloft heeft/ (Merckt:)
daerfe van niemandt anders in ghe-
holpen of ghedient en konden wor- **Pfal.49.8**
den.

Ende dat hy boven dien/ de felve
fyne Ghemeynte voor fijn affchepdt/
oock met ghetrouwe Dienaren/ A- **Eph.4.11**
poftelen/ Evangeliften/ Herders en- **Luc.10.1.**
de Leeraers (die hy met bidden ende
fmeecken/ door den Heyligen Gheeft **Lu.6.12.13**
ver-

verkozen hadde) beset heeft gelaten/
op datse de Ghemeynte regeren/ sijn
Joa.2.15. Kudde weyden/ daer over waecken/
voorstaen ende versorghen/ jae in alles doen souden gelijck hy haer voor-
ghegaen/gheleert/ghedaen ende haer
mat.28.20 belast heeft/ te leeren onderhouden al
dat hy haer bevolen hadde.

Dat oock desgelijcks d' Apostelen
daer nae/ als ghetrouwe Navolgers
1Tim.3.1 Christi/ ende Voorgangers der Ge-
meynte/ hier in neerstich gheweest
Act.1.23. zijn/ om met bidden ende smeecken
24 tot Godt/ door verkiesinge der broe-
Tit.1.5. deren/alle Steden/Plaetsen of Ghe-
meynten/ met Bisschoppen/ Her-
ders ende Voorganghers te versor-
ghen/ ende soodaenighe Persoonen
1.tim.4.16 daer toe te ordineren/die acht op haer
selven/ op de Leeringhe ende Kudde
Tit.2.1.2 mochten hebben/ die ghesondt in 't
Gheloove/ vroom van Leven ende
1Tim.3.7 Wandel/ende die soo wel buyten als
binnen der Ghemeynte/ van eenen
goeden Loff ende Gheruchte souden
zijn/

zijn/ op dat sy een Exempel/ Licht/
ende Voorbeeldt in alderley Godtsa-
lighheyt ende goede wercken mochten wesen/ en des Heeren Ordinan-
tien/ Doopsel en Avondtmael waer-
2Tim.2.2 delyck bedienen/ ende datse oock alder-weghen (daer sy te bekomen souden zyn) ghetrouwe Menschen/ bequaem om andere te leeren/tot Out-
1 tim.4.14 sten souden bestellen/ de selve met
ende 5.2. handt-opplegginge in den Naem des
Heeren bevestighen/ ende alle noodt-
saeckelijckheyt der Ghemeynte voorder versorghen naer vermoghen/ op
datse als ghetrouwe Knechten/haers
Luc.19.13 Heeren pondt wel regeeren/winnin-
ghe daer mede doen/ ende dien-volghens haer selven mochten behou-
den/ende die haer hoozen.

Ende datse oock neerstich waer-
nemen souden/ sonderlinghe elck onder den zynen/ daer hy opsicht over
Acto.6.3 heeft/ dat alle plaetsen met Diaken-
4.5.6. dienaren (om acht ende opsicht over
den Armen te houden) wel voorsien
C   ende

ende verforght moghen worden/ die
de Handt-repckinghe en Aelmoeffen
ontfanghen/ ende wederom aen den
armen Hepligen die nootdruftich
zpn/ ghetrouwelpck mogen uptdep-
len/ met alle eerbaerhepdt naer behooren.

1 Tim. 5.9
    Ende datmen oock Eerbare ou-
de Weduwen/ tot Dienareffen ordi-
neren ende verkiesen soude/ om neffens de Diaken-dienaren/ de arme
Rom. 16.1
Jac. 1.27.
swacke/ krancke/ bedroefde/ ende
nootdruftighe Menschen/ als oock
Weduwen en Weesen te besoecken/
te vertroosten en te verforghen/ ende
voorts de noodtfaeckelijckheydt der
Ghemepnte te helpen waer-nemen
na alle haer vermoghen.

    Ende wat noch voorder den Dia-
ken-dienaren aengaet/dat defelve bp-
fonder wanneer die bequaem/ ende
van der Ghemepnte daer toe verko-
ren ende verordineert worden(tot be-
hulp ende verlichtinghe der Outsten)
de Ghemepnte oock wel mogen ver-
manen/

manen/ende mede in 't Woordt ende
Leeringhe arbepden/ om peghelpck
alfoo den anderen upt Liefde te die-
nen/metter gave die hp van den Heere heeft ontfanghen: Op dat door
ghemepnen dienst/ ende handt-repckinghe van pder Lidt/ elck in zijnder
mate/ het Lichaem Christi gebetert/
ende des Heeré Wijnstock ende Ge-
mepnte in wasdom/ toe-neminghe
ende bouwinge magh blpven na behooren.

    Ten tienden/ soo bekennen ende
onderhouden wp mede een Broodt-
breeckinghe ofte Avondtmael/ ghelpck als de Heere Christus Jesus
Mt.26.25
Mr 14.22
Acto. 2.42
1Cor.10.6
1Co.11.22
voor sijn Lpden sulcks met Broodt
ende Wijn in-ghestelt/ ende oock
met sijn Apostelen selfs ghebrupckt
en ghegheten/ ende haer tot zijnder
gedachtenisse te onderhouden bevolen heeft/ ende ghelpck sp dien-volghens sulcks oock in der Ghemepnte gheleert/ beleeft/ ende den Gheloovighen belast ende bevolen hebben te

       C 2   onder-

onderhouden/tot ghedachteniſſe van
des Heeren Doot/Lyden en ſterven/
ende dat ſijn weerdige Lichaem voor
ons/ ende het gheheele menſchelijcke
gheſlachte ghebzoocken/ en ſijn dier-
baer Bloedt vergoten is: als oock
mede daer beneffens de vzucht van
dien/ namelijck de Verloſſinghe ende
eeuwighe Salighepdt/ dewelcke hp
daer dooz verwozven/ ende aen ons
ſondighe menſchen ſoodanighen liefde bewelen heeft: Waer dooz wp ten
hooghſten vermaendt wozden malkanderen ende onſen naeſten wederom lief te hebben/ vergeven en quijt-
ſchelden/ ghelpck hp ons ghedaen
heeft/ ende oock te ghedencken te on-

Act.2. 46. derhouden ende te beleven de Eenig-
hepdt ende Ghemepnſchap/ die wp
met Godt/ ende onder malkanderen
ſijn hebbende/dewelcke ende alſo ons
de ſelve/ bp ſulck bzeken des bzoots/
aengeweſen en betepckent wozdt.

Ten elfden/ bekennen ende belpden wp oock: Een Voet-waſſchin-
ghe

ghe der Heplighen/ ghelpck de Heere
Chziſtus ſulcks niet alleen in-geſtelt/
belaſt ende bevolen/ maer oock ſelfs
ſpne Apoſtelen (hoewel hp haer Heere ende Meeſter was) de voeten ghewaſſchen heeft/ ende daer mede een
Exempel ghegheven/ dat ſp van gelijcke malkanderen oock de Voeten
waſſchen ende alſoo doen ſouden/ge-
lijck als hp haer ghedaen hadde/ dat
welck ſp oock dien-volghende/ den
Gheloovighen om te onderhouden
voozt-gheleert hebben/ alles tot een
tepcken van ware vernederinge/ als
oock vooznamelick om bp deſe Voet-
waſſchinghe te ghedencken de rechte
waſſchinghe/ daer wp dooz ſijn dierbare Bloedt mede ghewaſſchen ende
na der zielen gherepnight zijn.

Ten twaelfden/ ſoo bekennen ende belpden wp in der Ghemepnte
Godts: Eenen eerlijcken Houwe-
lijcken-ſtaet/ van twee vzpe gheloovighe Perſoonen/ achtervolghende/
ende als Godt aenvanckelijck de ſel-

C 3   ve

Joſ.13.4.
tot óſ.17.
I Tim.5.10
Gen.18.4
Gen.19.2

Exempel.
Gen.8. 4.
ende 19:2.

Gen.1.26

Gen.2.22 be in den Paradijse geordineert/ende met Adam ende Eva selfs in-ghestelt heeft. Ende ghelijck de Heere Christus alle misbruyck des Houwelijcks/ middeler-tijdt in-ghekomen zijnde/

Mat.19.4 wech-ghenomen/af-gheleert/ende alles wederom op de eerste Ordeninge ghewesen ende daer by gelaten heeft/

1 Cor.7.* in welcker voegen den Apostel Paulus het Houwelijck oock inder Ghe-meynte gheleert/ toe-ghelaten/ ende een peghelijck vry ghestelt heeft/ om na de eerste Ordeninghe in den Hee-re te moghen trouwen/ aen wie/ende welcke men daer toe kan verwillige:

1.Cor.9.5 met welcke woorden [in den Heere]

Gen.24.* na onse meyninghe behoort verstaen te worden/dat/ghelijck als de Oudt-

Gen.28.* vaders/ aen haer Maeghschap/ oft Gheslachte moesten houwelijcken: dat oock in ghelijcker mate de Ghe-loovighe des Nieuwen Testaments gheen andere Vryheydt vergunt oft toe-ghelaten is / als om alleen onder dat uytverkozen Gheslachte/ en gee-stelijcke

stelijcke Maeghschap Christi te mo-ghen trouwen/ Namelijck aen den ghenen (en gheen andere) die eerst en al-vooren metter Ghemeynte als een herte ende ziele vereenight zijn/ een Doopsel ontfanghen hebben/ende in eenderley Ghemeynschap/ Ghelo-ve/ Leere en Belevinghe staen/al eer sy door den Houwelijcken-staet haer met malkander moghen vereenigen: De soodanighe (ghelijck verhaelt is) die worde dan na de eerste Ordenin-ghe van Godt in sijn Ghemeynte te samen gheboeght/ende dat is alsdan in den Heere trouwen. 1Cor.7.39

Ten dertienden/ soo gelooven/be-kennen en belijde wy oock: dat God de Macht ende de Overheydt geor-dineert heeft/ende gestelt tot straffin-ge over de quade/ ende beschermince der goede/en voorder om de werelt te regeren/Lande en Steden/als mede hare Onderdaten in goede Ordinan-tien ende Policien te onderhoude; en dat wy over sulcx de selve niet en mo- Rom.13.1 2.3.4.5.6. 7.

C 4   ghen

Titu.3.1. ghen verachten/ noch lasteren of wederstaen / maer dat wp haer moeten
1Pet.2.17 als een Dienaeresse Gods erkennen/
eeren/onderdanich ende gehooisaem/
ja tot alle goede wercken bereyt zijn/
bysonder in 't ghene niet tegen Gods
Wet/Wille en Gebodt is strydende ;
ende haer oock ghetrouwelijck Tol /
Mt 22.21 Excijns en Schattinghe te betalen/
en gheven dat haer toe-behooit/ghe-
lyck den Sone Gods gheleert / oock
Mt 17.27 selfs ghedaen / ende den sijnen belast
en bevolen heeft oock alsoo te doen :
Dat wp oock boven dien /den Heere
booi haer ende hare Welstandt/ende
1Ti.2.1.2 des Landts beste ghestadich en ernstelijck moeten bidden / op dat wp
onder hare Bescherminghe moghen
woonen / ons gheneeren / en een stil
gherust leven lepden met alder God-
salicheydt/ende eerlijckheydt/ Ende
booits / dat de Heere alle Weldaedt /
Vipheydt ende Gunst/dewelcke wp
hier onder hare Loffelijcke Regierin-
ghe ghenieten/ haer-lieden hier/ende
namaels

naemaels inder eeuwicheydt wil loo-
nen en vergelden.

   Ten veerthienden / aengaende de
Wiaecke / om de Vpanden met den
Sweerde te wederstaen : Wp ghelooven ende belpden / dat de Heere
Chiistus sijn Discipulen ende Nae- Mat 5.39
volghers / alle wiaecke ende weder- ende 44.
wiaecke verboden /ende af-gheleert
heeft / ende belast ende bevolen nie- rom 12.14
mandt quaet met quaet / noch vloeckinge met vloeckinge te verghelden/ 1.Pet. 3.9
maer het Sweerdt inde scheede te ste-
ken/ oft/als de Piopheten booisepdt Esai.2. 4.
hebben / Ploegh-psers daer van te Mich.4.3
maecken: Waer upt wp verstaen / Sach.9.8
dat ober sulcks / en achtervolghende 9.
sijn Exempel/ Leven en Leeringhe/
wp niemandt lpden/ leedt of verdiet
aen mogen doen/maer alle menschen
haer hoochste Welvaert ende Salig-
heydt behooien te soecken/ende oock
als't den noot berepscht om des Heeren wille te vluchten/van d'eene stadt
of landt in d' ander/ en beroobinghe
                  C 5   der

der goederen te lyden/maer niemant
mat. 5.39. lyden aen te doen/geslagen worden-
de/liever d'ander wange oock te bie-
nen/als hemselven te wreken oft wederom te slaen/en dat wy daer en bo-
rom.12.20 ven oock voor onse vyanden moeten
bidden/en wanneer sy hongerich oft
dorstich zijn/haer laven ende spysen/
om haer alsoo met wel-doen te over-
tuyghen/ende alle onwetenheydt te
verwinnen/eyndelijck dat wy moe-
2Cor.4.2. ten goet doen/ende ons wel bewysen
tegen alle Conscientien der menschē/
Mat.7.12 ende na de Wet Christi/niemant yet
anders moghen doen/als wy wilden
dat ons geschiede.

Ten vijfthienden/aengaende het
Eedt-sweeren/daer van ghelooven
eñ belyden wy: Dat de Heere Christus het selve mede den sijnen af-ghe-
Matth.5. leert ende verboden heeft/om in geen-
34.35. derley wijse niet te moghen sweeren/
Jac. 5.12. maer dat Jae/Jae/ende Neen/
Neen moet wesen: Waer uyt wy
verstaen/dat ons alle hooghe ende
leeghe

leeghe Eeden verboden zijn/maer
dat wy in plaetse van dien alle onse
beloften/toesegginghen ende verbin-
tenissen/jae oock alle onse verklarin-
ghen ofte ghetuyghenissen van eenighe saecken/alleen met onse woort
Jae/in't ghene dat Jae is/ende *2Cor.1.17*
Neen/in't ghene dat Neen is moeten
bevestigē/mits dat wy 't selve altoos
ende in alderley saecken neffens een
yeghelijck soo ghetrouwelijck moeten standt doen/onderhouden/ach-
tervolghen ende naekomen/als of
wy sulckx met hooghe Eeden bevesticht ende gheswooren hadden/
ende wanneer wy 't selve also doen/
so vertrouwen wy niet/dat yemant/
jae d'Overheydt selfs met reden oor-
saecke sal hebben/om ons in't ghemoedt en conscientie hoogher te be-
swaren.

Ten sesthienden soo ghelooven/
belyden ende bekennen wy oock eenen Ban/Afsonderinge ende Christelijcke Straffe inder Ghemeynte/
tot

tot beteringhe ende niet tot verder=
vinghe/ om daer door alsoo het reyne
van het onreyne te onderscheyden:
Namelijck/ wanneer yemandt nae
dat hy verlicht/ de kennisse der waer=
heydt aenghenomen/ ende in de ghe=
meynschap der Heylighen inghelijft
Esai.59.2 is/ ende daer nae wederom/ het zy
moetwillich/ oft uyt vermetenheydt
1 Cor.5.5 teghen Godt/ ofte anderssins totter
en vers.12
1 tim.5.20 doodt komt te sondighen/ ende in
soodanighe onvruchtbaere wercken
der duysternisse vervalt/ daer door
hy van Godt gheschepden ende hem
het Rijcke Godts afgheseydt wordt/
dat die selve dan/ nae dattet werck
openbaer ende der Ghemeynte ghe=
noegh bekent is/ niet en mach bly=
ven in de Vergaderinghe der Recht=
vaerdighen/ maer dat de selve als een
ergerlijck Lidt ende openbare Son=
1 tim.5.20 daer behoort/ ende moet afgesondert/
1.Cor.5.6 wech-ghedaen/ voor allen ghestraft/
en als een Suer-deegh uytgebaeght
2Cor.10.8 worden/ ende dat tot sijnder beterin=
2Co.13.10 ghe/

ghe/ tot een exempel ende vreese van
andere/ ende tot reyn-houdinghe der
Ghemeynte/ om de selve van sulcke
schandtvlecken te suyveren/ ende op
dat by ghebreecke van dien/ den
Name des Heeren daer door niet ge=
lastert/ de Ghemeynte onteert/ noch
die buyten sijn/ gheen aenstoot of er=
ghernisse ghegheven mochte worden/
eyndelijck/ op dat een Sondaer met=
ter weereldt niet verdoemt/ maer in
sijn ghemoedt overtuyght ende we=
derom tot berouw/ boete ende bete=
ringhe beweeght mochte worden.
Wat nu voorder aengaet de Broe=
derlijcke Straffe ofte Aenspraecke/
als oock om den doolenden te onder= Jac.5.19.
wijsen/ daer in behoordt oock alle
naerstigheydt gedaen/ en sorghe ghe=
draghen te worden/ om de selve waer
te nemen/ ende met alle sachtmoedig=
heydt ten besten te vermaenen/ tot
haerder beteringhe/ ende de hertnec= Tit.3.10.
kighe die onbekeerlijck blyven/ te
straffen/ nae behooren: Somma/
dat

1Cor.5.12 dat de Ghemeynte moet van haer wech-doen die daer quaedt is / (het sy in Leere of Leven) en niemandt anders.

Ten seventhienden aengaende de Ontreckinghe oft Mydinghe der afghesonderde / daer van ghelooven ende belyden wy : dat soo wanneer yemandt / het sy door sijn quade leven / of verkeerde leeringhe / soo verre komt te vervallen / dat hy van Godt afgheschepden / ende dien-volghens oock van der Ghemeynte recht afghesondert ende ghestraft is / dat die selve dan oock behoort ende volgens de Leere Christi / ende sijnder Apostelen/moet sonder onderschepdt/van alle Medeghenooten ende Lidtmaten der Ghemeynte (bysonder van de ghene die sulckx bekent is) het sy in Eten of Drincken / ende andere diergghelijcke Ghemeynschap / 1Corint. 5 9.10.11. gheschuwt ende ghemijdt worden / ende datmen daer mede niet te doen mach 2Tes.3.14 Tit.3.10. hebben : op datmen door haere conversa-

versatie niet besmet/noch hare Sonden niet deelachtigh en worde / maer dat den Sondaer beschaemt / in sijn ghemoedt gheraeckt/ende inde Conscientie/ tot zijnder beteringhe / overtuyght worden mochte/datter nochtans soo wel in der Mydinghe als inde Straffinghe / soodanighen mate ende Christelijcke beschepdenhept behoort ghebruyckt te worden / dat de selve niet tot verdervinghe / maer den Sondaer tot beteringhe magh dienen : want de selve nootdruftich/ hongerich/dorstich/ naeckt/ kranck/ ofte in eenich ander onghemack zijnde / soo zijn wy schuldich (de noodt vereyschende / volghens de Liefde ende oock nae de Leere Christi en sijnder Apostelen) haer-lieden noch evenwel hulpe en bystant te bewysen / anders soude de Mydinghe in sulcken gheballe / meer tot verdervinghe als tot beteringhe dienen; Over sulckx en moetmen haer niet houden als Ypanden / maer de selve ver- 2Tes.5.14

manen

manen als een Broeder / om daer
door tot kenniffe / berouw ende leet=
wefen van hare fonden te brenghen :
op dat fp haer met Godt ende ſijn
Ghemepnte wederom verfoenen / en
dien volgens weder in de Ghemepn=
te ontfanghen ende aen-ghenomen
moghen worden / ende dat de Liefde
aen haer den voortganck magh heb=
ben naer behooren.

Ten achtienden ende ter laetften/
aengaende de Verrijfeniffe der Doo=
den / daer van belpden wp metten
monde / ende ghelooven fulcks oock
metter herten nae der Schriftuere/
dat door de onbegrijpelicke kracht
Godts ten Jonghften daghe / alle
Menfchen die gheftorven ende ont=
flapen fullen zijn / alfdan wederom
opghewerckt / levendich ghemaeckt
worden / ende verrifen fullen / ende
dat de felve met den ghenen die dan
noch in't leven overghebleven fullen
zijn/ ende in een ooghenblick/ ter tijdt
der laetfter Bafupne verandert wor=
den/

den / te famen voor den Rechter-ftoel
Chrifti gheftelt / de goede en quade
van een ghefchepden fullen worden/
ende dat een pghelück dan in zijn
epghen lichaem ontfanghen fal nae
dat hp ghedaen heeft/het zp goet ofte
quaedt / ende dat de goede of vrome
als de gebenedijde/ alfdan met Chri=
fto opghenomen fullen worden/ ende
in't eeuwighe leven gaen / ende ont=
fanghen de vreuchde/ de welcke nopt
ooghe heeft ghefien / of oore gehoort/
noch is gheen Menfchen herte en is
gekomen / om met Chrifto te regne=
ren en triumpheren van eeuwichept
tot eeuwichepdt / Ende dat daer te=
ghen de quade of onvrome/ als ver=
maledijde / verwefen en verftooten
fullen worden / in de donckere dup=
fterniffe/ jae eeuwighe Helfche pijne/
daer haeren worm niet fterven noch
haer vper niet uptgeblufcht fal wor=
den / en daer fp (nae lupdt der hepli=
gher Schrift) gheen hope/ troost/
noch verlofſinghe te verwachten ful=
D   len

len hebben inder eeuwichepdt : De
Heere wil ons door sijn ghenaede/
altesamen weerdich en bequaem maken / dat sulckx onser gheen en mach
overkomen / maer dat wy ons selven
alsoo moghen waer-nemen en be-
neerstighen / om dan in dien tijdt
voor hem bevonden te moghen worden onbevleckt ende onstraffelijck in
den vrede/Amen.

Soo zijn dit nu als boven in 't korte vergaelt is/de principale Articulen
onses al-ghemeynen Christelijcken
Gheloofs/ ghelijck wy de selve alsoo
in onser Ghemeynte/ en onder den
onsen doorgaens leeren/ ende bele-
ven/ t'welck naer onse gheboelen/het
eenighe oprechte Christelijcke Gheloove is/ dat de Apostelen in haeren
rydt ghelooft ende gheleert/ jae 't selve met haer leven betuyght/met haeren doodt bevestight/en oock eenighe
met haer bloedt bezeghelt hebben/
daer wy neffens haer en alle vrome/
nae

nae onse zwackhepdt/oock gheerne
in souden blyben/ leven en sterven/
om met de selve door des Heeren ghe-
nade/namaels de Salichepdt te moghen verwerven.

Ende is besloten/ dat twee gelijck-
luydende/ en vp ons ghe-onderteyc-
kende/ als principale van desen/ sullen blyven berusten/ d'eene alhier tot
Dordrecht/ en d'ander tot Amster-
dam/ ende dat de selve vp alle de on-
dergeschreven Oudtsten/ die nu hier
vergadert zijn/sullen vpt-ghecopieert
ende Coppe met haer genomen wor-
den/ soo om de selve veghelijck in hare plaetse te vertoonen / als oock om
Coppe van dien voorder te bestellen
aen de Ghemeynte/ veghelijck onder zijn bedieninghe behoorende.

Ende naedien seer liebe ende be-
minde Mede-hulpers/ Broeders en
Susters/ en alle Mede-genooten in
Christo/ wy vertrouwen/ dat wy
vpt dese korte Schriftelijcke vertoo-
D 2   ninghe

ninghe / wel verstaen en begrppen
sult/onses werckx ende arbepts/aen=
gaende deser sake inder Liefden ghe=
daen ende gheschiedt. Oversulcks
soo versoecken ende bidden wp oot=
moedelijck en vriendelijck aen V. L.
dat ghp van ons onwaerdich doch
alles ten goeden wilt afnemen /'t sel=
ve inder Liefden wilt naebolghen/
ende sulckx u aenghenaem ende ge=
vallich/ tot uwen hooghsten Vrede
ende beteringhe onder malkanderen
laeten dienen : Op dat alsoo Godt
des Vreeds met V. L. en ons te sa=
men/ volghens zijn belofte/ sijn en
blpven / ende het goede begonnen
werck zpnen voozt-ganck hebben/
ende tot des Heeren prijs/ wasdom
ende bouwinghe sijnder Ghemepnte
dienen mach. Daer toe/en voozts tot
alles wat ons ten selven epnde/of an=
dersins noodich en vooz hem beha=
ghelijck is/wil ons en V.L. de goede
ghenadige barmhertige God helpen
zpnen

zpnen ghenaedighen zeghen verlee=
nen/ stercken/ bekrachtighen ende al
te samen waerdigh en bequaem ma=
ken/Amen.

Versoecken / bidden ende beghee=
ren oock gantsch vriendelijck aen al=
le / ende op een peghelijck in 't bpson=
der/die dese onse vooz-verhaelde ver=
tooninghe ter handt oft in kennisse
soude moghen bekomen/sien/hoozen
ofte lesen/ende nochtans 't selve in al=
len deelen niet en konden toestaen /
appzoberen oft naebolghen /dan in
sulcke gevalle/ doch immers niet an=
ders als het beste daer van te willen
spzeken/ende ghedencken datter ghe=
schzeven staet : Wie het beste tot ter
saecke spzeeckt / (ende alle dinck ten
besten upt-leght) van dien spzeeckt-
men wederom het beste; ende dat den
Soone Godts belast ende bevolen
heeft / alle wat ghp wilt dat de men=
schen u doen/ dat doet hen oock/ ende
sult wel doen.

Tot kennisse/ ghetupghenisse en=
D 3   de

de volkomen beveſtinghe/dat al-hier
by der Gemeynte/ende by ons buy-
ten-mannen/te ſamen ende met malkanderen alles alſoo verhandelt ende
geſchiedt is/als vozen verhaelt ſtaet:
Soo hebben wy onder-ghcſchzeven
Oudtſten/ Dienaren ende Bzoede-
ren ſulckx uyt den name van wegen
en dooz begheerte/ van deſe onſe als
nu vereenichde Ghemeynte alhier/
als oock ſoo vooz ons ſelven/ en van
wegen elcx onſe Gemeynte/ het ſelve
als onſe openbare en generale Bzoe-
derlijcke Vereeninge/Bevzedinge en
Verdzagh/ met onſe eyghen han-
dē onderſchzeven/ en ondertepckent.
Gebzuyckt het ten goeden/ ende zijt
hier mede Godt Almachtich in ſij-
ne ghenadighe bewaeringhe tot ſa-
lighepdt bevolen/ en van ons alteſa-
men ende bander Ghemeynte alhier
hertelijck ghegroet/ met des Heeren
eeuwighen Vzede/ Amen.

Aldus ghedaen ende gheepndight
binnen onſe vereenichde Ghemeynte
alhier

alhier/ in der Stadt Dozdzecht/ op
den 21.Apzil/A°. 1632. ſtylo novo.
Vaert wel.

Ende was ondertepckent

Dordrecht.	Dordrecht.
Iſack de Coningh. en van weghen onſe Diender Ian Iacobs.	Per my Hans Cobrijſſen. By my Iacuis Terwen. Claes Dirckſen. Mels Ghijsbaerts. Aeriaen Corneliſſoon.
Middelburgh.	
Baſtiaen Willemſen. Ian Winckelmans.	**Van boven in 't Lant.**
Vliſſinghen.	Peeter van Berſel. Antonij Hanſʒ.
Oillaert Willeborts. Per Iacob Pennen. Lieven Marijneſʒ.	**Krevelt dito.**
Amſterdam.	Herman op den Graff. Weylm Kreynen.
Tobias Govertſʒ. Pieter Ianſen Moijer. Abraham Dirokxſʒ.	**Zeelandt.**
Haerlem.	Cornelis de Moir. Iſaac Claeſſen.
Ian Doom. Pieter Grijſheer.	**Haerlem.**
Bommel.	Dirck Wouters Kolenkamp. Pieter Iooſten.
Willem Ianſen van Exſelt. Ghisbert Spiering.	**Rotterdam.**
Rotterdam.	Iſrael van Halmael. Heyndrick Dirckſʒ. Apel- doren.
Balten Centen Schoenmaker. Michiel Michielſʒ.	Andries Luckn, de jonghe. Schie-

Schiedam.
Cornelis Bom.
Lambrecht Paeldinck.

Leyden.
Mr.Christiaen de Coninck.
Ian Weyns.

Blockziel.
Claes Claeßen.
Pieter Peters.

Siericzee.
Anthuenis Cornelisz.
Pieter Iansen Timmerman.

Uytrecht.
Herman Segerts.
Ian Hendricksen Hoochvelt.
Daniel Lhorens.

Amsterdam.
David ter Haer.
Pieter Iansen van Singel.

Gorcum.
Iacob van den Heyde se-
brechts.
Ian Iansz. vande Cruysen.

Aernhem.
Cornelijes Iansen.
Derijck Rendersen.

Uytrecht.
Abraham Spronck.
Willem van Broeckhuysem.

EYNDE.

A List of the Editions
of the Dordrecht Confession of Faith
in the Original Dutch and in Translations

Since it first appeared in print in 1633, the Dordrecht Confession of Faith has gone through many editions, especially in German, English, and Spanish translations. The list below represents an effort to record these many editions both as they appeared in separate books and as part of a *Sammelband* or composite volume. The list is hardly complete in terms of the past as well as the present, for older editions are still not on record, and new editions constantly appear in print.

The information given here about the various editions is the bare minimum. We hope, however, that this information will serve as a guide to more complete identification: To the names of publishers and printers as well as translators. Equally important are the textual variants. We know, for example, that at least two editions printed in Switzerland had nineteen articles rather than the usual eighteen. (This list succeeds the trial list of 202 editions which appeared in *Doperse Stemmen*, no. 5 [Amsterdam: 1982], pp. 60-63.)

Although the list may assist librarians and collectors in their work, the chief purpose is to provide evidence of the widespread use of the Confession and to facilitate the historical and doctrinal study of its contents. Among the persons who assisted in gathering the information we especially acknowledge the help of Amos B. Hoover, David Luthy, Grace I. Showalter, Nelson P. Springer, and Dirk Visser.

Dutch

1. *Confessie ende vredehandelinge*. Haerlem: 1633.
2. *Confessie des Christelicken geloofs*. Rotterdam: 1658.
3. *Confessie van Dordrecht, 1632*. Doperse stemmen, no. 5. Amsterdam: 1982.
4. In: T. J. van Braght, *Het bloedigh Tooneel der Doops-geside en weerloose Christenen*. Dordrecht: 1660.
5. In: T. J. van Braght, *Het Bloedig Tooneel of Martelaers Spiegel*. Amsterdam: 1685.
6. In: T. J. van Braght, [Facsimile reprint of the 1685

edition]. Haarlem: 1984.

7. In: *Algemeene belydenissen der Doopsgezinde gemeynte Gods.* Amsterdam: 1665.

8. In: *Algemeene belydenissen der Doopsgezinde gemeynte Gods.* Haarlem: 1700.

9. In: *Algemeene belydenissen der Doopsgezinde gemeynte Gods.* Rotterdam: 1739.

10. In: *Handelinge der Ver-eenigde Doops-gesinde Gemeynten.* Vlissinghe: 1666.

German

The titles vary: *Christliche Glaubensbekentnus, Glaubensbekentnis des wehr-und rachlosen Christentums, Glaubens-Bekenntnis der Mennoniten,* and others.

11. *Christliche Glaubensbekentnus.* Amsterdam: 1664.

12. *Christliche Glaubensbekentnus.* Amsterdam: 1686.

13. *Christliche Glaubensbekentnus.* Amsterdam: 1691.

14. *Christliche Glaubensbekentnus.* [N.p.]: 1711.

15. *Christliche Glaubensbekentnus.* [N.p.]: 1742.

16. *Christliche Glaubensbekentnus.* Basel: 1822.

17. *Christliche Glaubensbekentnus.* Giessen: 1834.

18. *Christliche Glaubensbekentnus.* Zweibrücken: 1841.

19. *Christliche Glaubensbekentnus.* Rudnerweide: 1853.

20. *Christliche Glaubensbekentnus.* Zweibrücken: 1854.

21. *Christliche Glaubensbekentnus.* Mümpelgart: 1855.

22. *Christliche Glaubensbekentnus.* Mümpelgart: 1860.

23. *Christliche Glaubensbekentnus.* Regensburg: 1876.

24. *Christliche Glaubensbekentnus.* Elkhart, Indiana: 1878.

25. *Christliche Glaubensbekentnus.* Elkhart: 1899.

26. *Christliche Glaubensbekentnus.* Mountain Lake, Minnesota: [N.d.].

27. *Christliche Glaubensbekentnus.* Moundridge, Kansas: [N.d.].

28. *Christliche Glaubensbekentnus.* Baltic, Ohio: 1958.

29. *Christliche Glaubensbekentnus.* Kalona, Iowa: 1970.

30. *Christliche Glaubensbekentnus.* Arthur, Illinois: 1970.

31. *Christliche Glaubensbekentnus.* Baltic: [1970].

32. *Christliche Glaubensbekentnus.* Baltic: [1972].

33. *Christliche Glaubensbekentnus.* Baltic: [1975].

34. *Christliche Glaubensbekentnus.* Baltic: [N.d.].

35. *Christliche Glaubensbekentnus.* Baltic: 1983.

36. In: T. J. v. Braght. *Martyrer-Spiegel.* Ephrata: 1748-1749.

37. In: T. J. v. Braght. *Martyrer-Spiegel.* Pirmasens: 1780.

38. In: T. J. v. Braght. *Martyrer-Spiegel.* Lancaster: 1814.

39. In: T. J. v. Braght. *Martyrer-Spiegel.* Philadelphia: 1849.

40. In: T. J. v. Braght. *Martyrer-Spiegel.* Elkhart: 1870.

41. In: T. J. v. Braght. *Martyrer-Spiegel.* Scottdale: 1915.

42. In: T. J. v. Braght. *Martyrer-Spiegel.* Berne, Indiana: 1950.

43. In: T. J. v. Braght. *Martyrer-Spiegel.* Scottdale: 1962.

44. In: T. J. v. Braght. *Martyrer-Spiegel*. Aylmer, Ontario: 1967.

45. In: T. J. v. Braght. *Martyrer-Spiegel*. Aylmer: 1973.

46. In: T. J. v. Braght. *Martyrer-Spiegel*. Aylmer: 1973 [1981].

47. In: *Güldene Aepffel in silbern Schalen*. [Basel]: 1702.

48. In: *Güldene Aepffel in silbern Schalen*. [Basel]: 1742.

49. In: *Güldene Aepffel in silbern Schalen*. [Basel]: 1742.

50. In: *Güldene Aepffel in silbern Schalen*. Ephrata: 1745.

51. In: *Anabaptisticum et Enthusiasticum*. [N.p.]: 1702.

52. In: G. Roosen. *Christliches Gemüthsgespräch*. Ephrata: 1769.

53. In: G. Roosen. *Christliches Gemüthsgespräch*. Ephrata: 1770.

54. In: G. Roosen. *Christliches Gemüthsgespräch*. Germantown: 1790.

55. In: G. Roosen. *Christliches Gemüthsgespräch*. Lancaster: 1811.

56. In: G. Roosen. *Christliches Gemüthsgespräch*. Lancaster: 1836.

57. In: G. Roosen. *Christliches Gemüthsgespräch*. Berlin, Ontario: 1839.

58. In: G. Roosen. *Christliches Gemüthsgespräch*. Doylestown, Pa.: 1848.

59. In: G. Roosen. *Christliches Gemüthsgespräch*. Elkhart: 1868.

60. In: G. Roosen. *Christliches Gemüthsgespräch*. Lancaster: 1869.

61. In: G. Roosen. *Christliches Gemüthsgespräch*. Elkhart: 1873.

62. In: G. Roosen. *Christliches Gemüthsgespräch*. Berlin: 1891.

63. In: G. Roosen. *Christliches Gemüthsgespräch*. Elkhart: 1902.

64. In: G. Roosen. *Christliches Gemüthsgespräch*. Kitchener, Ontario: 1919.

65. In: G. Roosen. *Christliches Gemüthsgespräch*. Scottdale: 1930.

66. In: G. Roosen. *Christliches Gemüthsgespräch*. Scottdale: 1972.

67. In: *Die ernsthafte Christenpflicht*. Ephrata: 1785.

68. In: *Die ernsthafte Christenpflicht*. Ephrata: 1808.

69. In: *Die ernsthafte Christenpflicht*. Somerset, Pa.: 1810.

70. In: *Die ernsthafte Christenpflicht*. Wooster, Ohio: 1826.

71. In: *Die ernsthafte Christenpflicht*. Lancaster: 1826.

72. In: *Die ernsthafte Christenpflicht*. Lancaster: 1841.

73. In: *Die ernsthafte Christenpflicht*. Berlin: 1846.

74. In: *Die ernsthafte Christenpflicht*. Lancaster: 1852.

75. In: *Die ernsthafte Christenpflicht*. Lancaster: 1862.

76. In: *Die ernsthafte Christenpflicht*. Lancaster: 1868.

77. In: *Die ernsthafte Christenpflicht*. Lancaster: 1875.

78. In: *Die ernsthafte Christenpflicht*. Berlin: 1878.

79. In: *Die ernsthafte Christenpflicht*. Elkhart: 1886.

80. In: *Die ernsthafte Christenpflicht*. Lancaster: 1892.

81. In: *Die ernsthafte Christenpflicht*. Elkhart: 1894.

82. In: *Die ernsthafte Christenpflicht*. Lancaster: 1904.

83. In: *Die ernsthafte Christenpflicht*. Elkhart: 1907.

84. In: *Die ernsthafte Christenpflicht*. Berlin: 1908.

85. In: *Die ernsthafte Christenpflicht*. Elkhart: 1914.

86. In: *Die ernsthafte Christenpflicht*. Scottdale: 1915.

87. In: *Die ernsthafte Christenpflicht*. Arthur, Illinois: 1921.

88. In: *Die ernsthafte Christenpflicht*. Scottdale: 1924.

89. In: *Die ernsthafte Christenpflicht*. Lancaster: 1927.

90. In: *Die ernsthafte Christenpflicht*. Scottdale: 1937.

91. In: *Die ernsthafte Christenpflicht*. Lancaster: 1939.

92. In: *Die ernsthafte Christenpflicht*. Kutztown, Pa.: 1941.

93. In: *Die ernsthafte Christenpflicht*. Scottdale: 1943.

94. In: *Die ernsthafte Christenpflicht*. Scottdale: 1945.

95. In: *Die ernsthafte Christenpflicht*. Lancaster, 1945.

96. In: *Die ernsthafte Christenpflicht*. Kitchener: 1952.

97. In: *Die ernsthafte Christenpflicht*. Scottdale: 1953.

98. In: *Die ernsthafte Christenpflicht*. Lancaster: 1953.

99. In: *Die ernsthafte Christenpflicht*. Scottdale: 1955.

100. In: *Die ernsthafte Christenpflicht*. Scottdale: 1958.

101. In: *Die ernsthafte Christenpflicht*. Lancaster: 1961.

102. In: *Die ernsthafte Christenpflicht*. Scottdale: 1961.

103. In: *Die ernsthafte Christenpflicht*. Lancaster: 1964.

104. In: *Die ernsthafte Christenpflicht*. Scottdale: 1965.

105. In: *Die ernsthafte Christenpflicht*. Scottdale: 1967.

106. In: *Die ernsthafte Christenpflicht*. Lancaster: 1968.

107. In: *Die ernsthafte Christenpflicht*. Scottdale: 1971.

108. In: *Die ernsthafte Christenpflicht*. Lancaster: 1972.

109. In: *Die ernsthafte Christenpflicht*. Scottdale, 1974.

110. In: *Die ernsthafte Christenpflicht*. Scottdale: 1975.

111. In: *Die ernsthafte Christenpflicht*. Lancaster: 1976.

112. In: *Die ernsthafte Christenpflicht*. Scottdale: 1978.

113. In: *Die ernsthafte Christenpflicht*. [Milverton, Ontario: 1979].

114. In: *Die ernsthafte Christenpflicht*. Scottdale: 1980.

115. In: *Die ernsthafte Christenpflicht*. Scottdale: 1982.

116. In: *Die ernsthafte Christenpflicht*. Scottdale: 1984.

117. In: *Die ernsthafte Christenpflicht*. Scottdale: 1986.

118. In: Benjamin Eby. *Kurzgefasste Kirchen Geschichte*. Berlin: 1841.

119. In: Benjamin Eby. *Kurzgefasste Kirchen Geschichte*. Lancaster: 1853.

120. In: Benjamin Eby. *Kurzgefasste Kirchen Geschichte*. Elkhart: 1868.

121. In: Benjamin Eby. *Kurzgefasste Kirchen Geschichte*. Elkhart: 1879.

122. In: Benjamin Eby. *Kurzgefasste Kirchen Geschichte*. Elkhart: 1901.

123. In: Benjamin Eby. *Kurzgefasste Kirchen Geschichte*. Kitchener: 1919.

124. In: Benjamin Eby. *Kurzgefasste Kirchen Geschichte*. Scottdale: 1936.

125. In: Benjamin Eby. *Kurzgefasste Kirchen Geschichte*. Scottdale: [1974].

126 In: Daniel K. Cassel. *Geschichte der Mennoniten*. Philadelphia: 1890.

French

127. *[Confession de foi chrétienne*. Amsterdam: ca. 1660.].

128. *Confession de foi chrétienne*. [N.p.]: 1771.

129. *Confession de foi chrétienne*. Nancy: 1862.

130. In: P. Widmer & J. H. Yoder. *Principes et Doctrines Mennonites*. Montbéliard & Bruxelles: 1955.

131. In: C. Mathiot & R. Boigeol. *Recherches Histo-*

riques sur les Anabaptistes. Flavion (Belgique):
1969.

English

The titles vary: *The Christian Confession of the Faith, The Confession of Faith, Mennonite Confession of Faith, Dordrecht Confession of Faith*.

132. *The Christian Confession of the Faith*. Amsterdam:
1712.

133. *The Christian Confession of the Faith*. Philadelphia: 1727.

134. *The Christian Confession of the Faith*. New Market, Virginia: 1810.

135. *The Christian Confession of the Faith*. Niagara, New York: 1811.

136. *The Christian Confession of the Faith*. Doylestown:
1814.

137. *The Christian Confession of the Faith*. West Chester: 1835.

138. *The Christian Confession of the Faith*. Skippackville: 1836.

139. *The Christian Confession of the Faith*. Scottdale:
1927.

140. *The Christian Confession of the Faith*. Scottdale:
1930.

141. *The Christian Confession of the Faith*. Scottdale:
1931.

142. *The Christian Confession of the Faith*. [Stouffville]:
1935.

143. *The Christian Confession of the Faith*. Scottdale:
1939.

144. *The Christian Confession of the Faith*. [Stouffville]:
1940.

145. *The Christian Confession of the Faith*. Scottdale:
1941.

146. *The Christian Confession of the Faith*. Scottdale:
1945.

147. *The Christian Confession of the Faith*. Scottdale:
1946.

148. *The Christian Confession of the Faith*. [Kitchener]:
1948.

149. *The Christian Confession of the Faith*. Scottdale:
1952.

150. *Confession of Faith*. St. Joe, Arkansas: [about 1954].

151. *The Christian Confession of the Faith*. Scottdale:
1957.

152. *The Christian Confession of the Faith*. Aylmer/ LaGrange: [1960].

153. *The Christian Confession of the Faith*. Hesston:
1961.

154. *The Christian Confession of the Faith*. Scottdale:
1963.

155. *The Christian Confession of the Faith*. Aylmer/ LaGrange: [1964].

156. *Mennonite Confession of Faith*. Hartville, Ohio:
1964.

157. *The Christian Confession of the Faith*. Crockett, Kentucky: 1965.

158. *The Christian Confession of the Faith*. Hesston:
1965.

159. *The Christian Confession of the Faith*. Crockett:
1966.

160. *The Christian Confession of the Faith*. [Kitchener:
1966].

161. *The Christian Confession of the Faith.* Aylmer/ LaGrange: [1967].

162. *The Christian Confession of the Faith.* Crockett: 1971.

163. *The Christian Confession of the Faith.* Crockett: 1975.

164. *The Christian Confession of the Faith.* Aylmer/ LaGrange: [1976].

165. *The Christian Confession of the Faith.* Warsaw, Indiana: 1976.

166. *The Christian Confession of the Faith.* Ste. Anne, Manitoba: 1977.

167. *The Christian Confession of the Faith.* [Kitchener: 1978].

168. *The Christian Confession of the Faith.* Crockett: 1979.

169. *The Christian Confession of the Faith.* Aylmer/ LaGrange: 1982.

170. *The Christian Confession of the Faith.* Minerva, Ohio: 1981.

171. *The Christian Confession of the Faith.* Minerva, Ohio: 1981.

172. *The Christian Confession of the Faith.* Aylmer/ LaGrange: 1984.

173. In: T. J. van Braght. *Martyrs Mirror.* Lancaster: 1836.

174. In: T. J. van Braght. *Martyrs Mirror.* Lancaster: 1837.

175. In: T. J. van Braght. *Martyrs Mirror.* Elkhart: 1886.

176. In: T. J. van Braght. *Martyrs Mirror.* Scottdale: 1938.

177. In: T. J. van Braght. *Martyrs Mirror.* Scottdale: 1950.

178. In: T. J. van Braght. *Martyrs Mirror.* Scottdale: 1951.

179. In: T. J. van Braght. *Martyrs Mirror.* Scottdale: 1964.

180. In: T. J. van Braght. *Martyrs Mirror.* Scottdale: 1968.

181. In: T. J. van Braght. *Martyrs Mirror.* Scottdale: 1972.

182. In: T. J. van Braght. *Martyrs Mirror.* Scottdale: 1975.

183. In: T. J. van Braght. *Martyrs Mirror.* Scottdale: 1977.

184. In: T. J. van Braght. *Martyrs Mirror.* Scottdale: 1979.

185. In: T. J. van Braght. *Martyrs Mirror.* Scottdale: 1982.

186. In: T. J. van Braght. *Martyrs Mirror.* Scottdale, 1985.

187. In: *Christian Spiritual Conversation.* Lancaster: 1857.

188. In: *Christian Spiritual Conversation.* Lancaster: 1870.

189. In: *Christian Spiritual Conversation.* Lancaster: 1878.

190. In: *Christian Spiritual Conversation.* Lancaster: 1892.

191. In: *Christian Spiritual Conversation.* Union Grove, Pa.: 1921.

192. In: *Christian Spiritual Conversation.* Scottdale: 1941.

193. In: *Christian Spiritual Conversation.* [Berne, Ind.:

1959].

194. In: *Christian Spiritual Conversation*. Philadelphia: 1974.

195. In: *Christian Spiritual Conversation*. [Quarryville, Pa.]: 1984.

196. In: Daniel K. Cassel. *History of the Mennonites*. Philadelphia: 1888.

197. In: I. Daniel Rupp. *An Original History of the Religious Denominations*. Philadelphia/Harrisburg: 1844.

198. In: [I. Daniel Rupp]. *History of All the Religious Denominations*. Harrisburg: 1848.

199. In: [I. Daniel Rupp]. *The Religious Denominations in the United States*. Philadelphia: 1859.

200. In: J. S. Hartzler & D. Kauffman. *Mennonite Church History*. Scottdale: 1905.

201. In: M. Gingerich. *The Mennonites in Iowa*. Iowa City: 1939.

202. In: J. C. Wenger, *History of the Mennonites of the Franconia Conference*. Telford: 1937.

203. In: J. C. Wenger, *The Doctrines of the Mennonites*. Scottdale: 1950.

204. In: W. L. Lumpkin. *Baptist Confessions of Faith*. Chicago: 1959.

205. In: J. H. Leith. *Creeds of the Church*. Garden City, N.Y.: 1963.

206. In: J. H. Leith. *Creeds of the Church*. Oxford, England: 1973.

207. In: *Mennonite Church Polity*. Scottdale: 1944.

208. In: *Mennonite Church Polity*. Scottdale: 1952.

209. In: *Confession of Faith and Ministers Manual*. Elkhart: 1890.

210. In: *Confession of Faith and Ministers Manual*. Elkhart: 1895.

211. In: *Confession of Faith and Ministers Manual*. Elkhart, 1900.

212. In: *Confession of Faith and Ministers Manual*. Elkhart: 1906.

213. In: *Confession of Faith and Ministers Manual*. Elkhart: 1914.

214. In: *Confession of Faith and Ministers Manual*. Elkhart: 1917.

215. In: *Confession of Faith and Ministers Manual*. Scottdale: 1925.

216. In: *Confession of Faith and Ministers Manual*. Scottdale: 1930.

217. In: *Confession of Faith and Ministers Manual*. Scottdale: 1942.

218. In: *Confession of Faith and Ministers Manual*. Scottdale: 1952.

219. In: *Confession of Faith and Ministers Manual*. [Moundridge: 1958].

220. In: *Confession of Faith and Ministers Manual*. [Moundridge: 1962].

221. In: *Confession of Faith and Ministers Manual*. Scottdale: 1968.

222. In: *Confession of Faith and Ministers Manual*. Ste. Anne, Man.: 1977.

223. In: *Confession of Faith and Ministers Manual*. Scottdale: 1979.

224. In: *Doctrinal Statement, Ohio & Eastern Conference*. [n.p.]: 1938.

225. In: *Doctrinal Statement, Franconia Mennonite Conference*. Scottdale: 1947.

226. In: *Doctrinal Statement, Franconia Mennonite Conference.* Scottdale: 1957.
227. In: *A Devoted Christian's Prayer Book.* [Daviess Co., Ind.: 1964].
228. In: *A Devoted Christian's Prayer Book.* Aylmer/LaGrange: 1967.
229. In: *A Devoted Christian's Prayer Book.* Aylmer/LaGrange: 1976.
230. In: *A Devoted Christian's Prayer Book.* Aylmer/LaGrange: 1984.
231. In: Benjamin Eby. *A Concise Ecclesiastical History and Doctrinal Theology of the Baptists or Mennonites.* [N.p.: ca. 1941].
232. In: J. C. Wenger. *Glimpses of Mennonite History.* Scottdale: 1940.
233. In: J. C. Wenger. *Glimpses of Mennonite History.* Scottdale: 1947.
234. In: J. C. Wenger. *Glimpses of Mennonite History.* Scottdale: 1949.
235. In: J. C. Wenger. *Glimpses of Mennonite History.* Scottdale: 1959.
236. In: Menno Sauder. *A Christian Confession.* [Elmira, Ont.]: 1943.
237. In Menno Sauder. *A Christian Confession.* [Elmira]: 1945.
238. In: Menno Sauder. *The Christian Faith.* [Elmira]: 1945.
239. In: Menno Sauder. *Companion of a Solution.* [Elmira]: 1945.
240. In: Menno Sauder. *The True and False Church.* [Elmira]: 1944.
241. In: Menno Sauder. *The True and False Church.* 2nd ed. [Elmira]: 1944.
242. In: Menno Sauder. *The True and False Church.* [Elmira]: 1945.
243. In: Menno Sauder. *The Golden Truth.* [Elmira]: 1965.
244. In: Menno Sauder. *The Golden Truth.* [Elmira]: 1966.
245. In: Amos B. Hoover. *The Jonas Martin Era.* Denver, Pa.: 1982.
246. In: Howard John Loewen. *One Lord, One Church, One Hope, and One God.* Elkhart: 1985.
247. In: R. W. Grant. *A Field Study of the Amish.* Columbia, Mo.: 1968.
248. *A Mennonite Confession of Faith.* Bo-Bo Valley via Ulong, Australia: [1969?].

Spanish
249. In: J. C. Wenger. *Compendio de historica doctrina Menonita.* Scottdale: 1947.
250. In: J. C. Wenger. *Compendio de historica doctrina Menonita.* Scottdale: 1949.
251. In: J. C. Wenger. *Compendio de historica doctrina Menonita.* Scottdale: 1960.
252. In: *Confessión de fe y brefe catecismo* [Pehuajó, Argentina]: 1927.
253. In: *Una declaracion de la doctrina christiano.* [Moundridge: 1958].
254. *Confesiones de la fe Menonita* [Probably Honduras: ca. 1970].
255. *Confession de la fe christiana de la Iglesia Mennonita.* Farmington, New Mexico: 1981.